Series/Number 07-122

D0839846

College Library

GAME THEORY TOPICS

Incomplete Information, Repeated Games, and *N*-Player Games

EVELYN C. FINK
University of Nebraska–Lincoln

SCOTT GATES
Michigan State University

BRIAN D. HUMES
University of Nebraska–Lincoln

SAGE PUBLICATIONS
The International Professional Publishers
Thousand Oaks   London   New Delhi

Copyright ©1998 by Sage Publications, Inc.

All rights reserved. No part of this book may be reproduced or utilized in any form or by any means, electronic or mechanical, including photocopying, recording, or by any information storage and retrieval system, without permission in writing from the publisher.

For information:

SAGE Publications, Inc.
2455 Teller Road
Thousand Oaks, California 91320
E-mail: order@sagepub.com

SAGE Publications Ltd.
6 Bonhill Street
London EC2A 4PU
United Kingdom

SAGE Publications India Pvt. Ltd.
M-32 Market
Greater Kailash I
New Delhi 110 048 India

Printed in the United States of America

Library of Congress Cataloging-in-Publication Data

Fink, Evelyn C.
  Game theory topics: Incomplete information, repeated games, and N-player games / Evelyn C. Fink, Scott Gates, Brian D. Humes.
      p.   cm. — (Quantitative applications in the social sciences ; v. 122)
    Includes bibliographical references.
    ISBN 0-7619-1016-6 (pbk. : alk. paper)
    1. Game theory.   I. Gates, Scott.   II. Humes, Brian D.   III. Title.
  IV. Series: Sage university papers series.
  Quantitative applications in the social sciences ; no. 122.
  QA269.F485   1998
  519.3—dc21   98-14888

This book is printed on acid-free paper.

98 99 00 01 02 03 10 9 8 7 6 5 4 3 2 1

Acquiring Editor:	C. Deborah Laughton
Editorial Assistant:	Eileen Carr
Production Editor:	Astrid Virding
Typesetter:	Technical Typesetting, Inc.
Print Buyer:	Anna Chin

When citing a university paper, please use the proper form. Remember to cite the Sage University Paper series title and include paper number. One of the following formats can be adapted (depending on the style manual used):

(1) FINK, E. C., GATES, S., and HUMES, B. D. (1998) *Game Theory Topics: Incomplete Information, Repeated Games, and N-Player Games*. Sage University Papers Series on Quantitative Applications in the Social Sciences, 07-122. Thousand Oaks, CA: Sage.

OR

(2) Fink, E. C., Gates, S., & Humes, B. D. (1998). *Game theory topics: Incomplete information, repeated games, and N-player games* (Sage University Papers Series on Quantitative Applications in the Social Sciences, series no. 07-122). Thousand Oaks, CA: Sage.

QA
269
.F485
1998

O 70798 | 1153 M

CONTENTS

SERIES EDITOR'S INTRODUCTION

Interest in game theory has grown, beyond economics to the other social sciences. Games—players following rules for payoffs—are ancient, in both their recreational and serious forms. A gambler in the Wild West may win at poker and lose a gunfight. Understanding the rules of the game and their proper application has behavioral consequences. More generally, important aspects of social and political behavior may be explained or predicted. With respect to the formal study of game theory, our series has published one paper: an introduction by Zagare (*Game Theory*, No. 41). The work at hand builds on that earlier effort and covers current topics in the field. The treatment is at an intermediate level, generally focusing on the problems encountered in moving from normal form to extensive form games. Three kinds are explored: imperfect and incomplete information games, repeated games, and N-player games.

The authors use continuous examples to illustrate the dilemmas of each game. The primary example comes from the Chicken game, made famous in the classic film, *Rebel Without a Cause*. Two teenage toughs race their jalopies to cliff's edge, the first who jumps to save himself is "chicken." The bare-bones choices of the Chicken game appear, perhaps less dramatically, in many social and political decision-making situations. To convince us of this point, the authors develop the secondary example of the interaction of General Motors (GM) and Ford over lobbying contributions to limit pollution controls under the Clean Air Act of 1990. The two firms face the basic choice of contributing or not. The decision becomes more complicated as the rules of the game change. What if information is imperfect? That is, no player knows the moves of the other, but still must move. The change to imperfect information alters the game's equilibria.

In real life, most games are repeated, rather than single shot. For instance, GM and Ford continue to interact over the air pollution issue. The notion of a repeated game allows Player 1 to take into account the past decisions of Player 2. However, this complicates the determination of equilibrium, that state where each player is getting as much as he or she can, given obtainable information and the choices the other players are making. An additional wrinkle is that repeated games may be finite or infinite. The latter may be more realistic; for example, GM and Ford may go back and forth indefinitely over pollution control issues. With the situation of the infinitely repeated game, opportunities for cooperation are most likely to arise, but now there are very many ways to get to an equilibrium, as the Folk theorem reminds us. The equilibria are also changed when a third player, such as Chrysler, is added. This is a case of the more general problem of the N-player game, discussed in the last chapter.

More and more, veteran researchers are exploring sophisticated game theory approaches to the study of politics and society. Methodology instructors confront the difficulty of what to assign their graduate students, beyond the few highly technical, costly, and full-fledged textbooks. Once the interested user has mastered the basics of game theory, this monograph by Professors Fink, Gates, and Humes, seems a good next step.

—*Michael S. Lewis-Beck*
Series Editor

ACKNOWLEDGMENTS

Evelyn C. Fink would like to thank William B. Heller and Valerie Schwebach for their comments. Scott Gates thanks Han Dorussen and Mark Jones for their helpful suggestions and his students, Andrew Padon, Dave Lektzian, Sara Benesh, and Mark Souva, for their comments. Brian D. Humes acknowledges the support of a summer fellowship from the Department of Political Science at the University of Nebraska-Lincoln and the Congress Fund of the University of Nebraska Foundation. He would also like to thank the students in his game theory class at the University of Nebraska-Lincoln during the Spring semester in 1997. He would especially like to acknowledge the comments of Daniel Brox, Sheng-Ping Yang, and Albert Van Cleef. Lastly, the authors would like to thank Michael Lewis-Beck, the series editor, and his two reviewers of the manuscript: Paul Johnson at the University of Kansas and one anonymous reviewer.

To my parents, from Scott
and
To Nathaniel, from Evelyn and Brian

PREFACE

Since the publication in this series of Frank Zagare's *Game Theory: Concepts and Applications* (1984), the field of game theory has grown greatly. For example, the standard game theory text used throughout the social sciences for over 20 years was Luce and Raiffa's *Games and Decisions* (1957). In recent years, this text has been replaced by various texts ranging in difficulty from Ordeshook's *Game Theory and Political Theory* (1986) to Myerson's *Game Theory: Analysis of Conflict* (1991). These texts contain more than just more applications of game theory. Instead, they illustrate how the field has expanded. The purpose of this monograph is to acquaint the uninitiated with some of the techniques that have been developed since the publication of Zagare's monograph. Specifically, we focus on three topics: the role of incomplete information, the role of repetition, and N-person games.

Innovations in these areas have allowed social scientists to model wide classes of situations that could not be analyzed before with game-theoretic models. Games of incomplete information allow us to consider situations where a player does not know with certainty the payoffs of another player. Repeated games allow us to examine situations where players interact over time. Finally, N-person games allow us to examine situations where more than two actors interact.

In writing this monograph, we assumed that the reader is familiar with the information developed in Chapters 1 and 3 of Zagare's monograph.[1] Readers should be familiar with terms such as extensive form games, normal form games, perfect information, imperfect information, complete information, incomplete information, and Nash equilibria. If these terms are unfamiliar, we strongly advise the reader to examine the above-mentioned chapters of Zagare's monograph or some other source.[2]

As previously noted, the objective of this monograph is to present developments in game theory in three areas. To achieve this goal, the manuscript is organized in the following manner. Chapter 1 provides a brief introduction to the use of game theory in the social sciences. This introduction is not meant to be a comprehensive review of applications of game theory. Rather, it is used to illustrate how game theory can be productively applied to problems in the social sciences.

Chapter 2 introduces readers to games of incomplete information. The discussion is both theoretical as well as substantively driven. We illustrate how the concept of incomplete information allows us to build uncertainty into game-theoretic models. We also discuss the concept of Bayesian Nash equilibrium. To develop the concept of incomplete information, we focus on a game that is common to the social sciences, that is, Chicken. We have chosen to focus on this "toy" game because of its widespread applications throughout the social sciences. It also provides an alternative to the more commonly used Prisoners' Dilemma game. The game of Chicken will be used throughout the text to illustrate the concepts being presented.

Chapter 3 introduces the reader to the role of repetition in game theory. We assume that the reader will be familiar with the work of Axelrod (1981). Our discussion will go well beyond this work to consider how different forms of repetition affect the equilibria of the game. We consider finitely repeated games, infinitely repeated games, and finitely repeated games with an unknown stopping point. In addition, we examine the role of discounting in the development of equilibria in repeated games. We also develop a simple version of the Folk theorem to illustrate the affect of repetition on the number of equilibria in the game. We show how repetition affects the possible outcomes that can be arrived at in Chicken.

Chapter 4 introduces readers to N-person noncooperative game theory. Our focus is to illustrate that game theory need not be limited to two or three players. We illustrate how game-theoretic models can easily accommodate many players. Once again, the lessons to be learned from this chapter are illustrated by expanding Chicken from its traditional two-person form to an N-person variation.

Throughout each of these chapters, we will also illustrate the concepts introduced in a particular chapter with applications to social sciences problems. These applications are used to help illustrate the points being developed in the particular chapter. They are not developed as an exhaustive treatment of some subject, but rather as an introduction.

GAME THEORY TOPICS
Incomplete Information, Repeated Games, and *N*-Player Games

EVELYN C. FINK
University of Nebraska–Lincoln

SCOTT GATES
Michigan State University

BRIAN D. HUMES
University of Nebraska–Lincoln

1. GAME THEORY: HOW IT IS USED

Overview

A common lament among social scientists when they begin to learn about game theory is: "How can this be applied to the real world?" This concern does not address the subject matter to which game theory is applied, but how one goes about applying it. This is the topic of this chapter. Game theory can be used in one of three manners. First, game theory is used to explore theoretical problems that arise directly from the development of game theory. For example, much time and effort went into explaining how one could get cooperation to arise in a Prisoners' Dilemma game. The motivation for such expenditure of resources came from the fact that social scientists observed situations in the real world that resembled the Prisoners' Dilemma where the actors cooperated instead of defected. Their question was what factors lead to such cooperation given that our theory does not predict this result. In other words, what major details are we missing in our models?

Second, game theory has been used to analyze actual strategic interactions in order to either predict or explain the actions of the actors involved. This type of analysis can be roughly divided into two camps. The first camp examines more general questions. For example, how can a leader get a follower to do what he wants her to do or, how effective are sanctions in international relations? The second camp examines specific cases. For example, why did the United States and New Zealand act in such a manner as to cause the informal breakup of ANZUS (Australia, New Zealand, United States alliance) or why did the United States and Pakistan follow certain policies vis-à-vis one another during the 1970s and 1980s?

Third, game theory has been used to analyze the logical consistency of certain arguments. For example, given their assumptions, are different theories of sanctions really inconsistent? Are various models of crisis bargaining and extended deterrence consistent with their hypotheses?

In this chapter, we will provide examples of how game theory has been used in each of these three manners. Our specific examples are discussed in the following order. First, we examine the theoretical problems that were addressed by Axelrod (1981). Then we examine generic problems of leadership along with specific applications (Calvert, 1987). Finally, we examine work by Morrow (1989) on the logical consistency of various empirical models of crisis bargaining and extended deterrence.

In writing the following sections of this chapter, the authors have assumed that the readers have an elementary understanding of game theory. However, jargon and game-theoretic representations have been kept to a minimum.

Addressing Theoretical Concerns

Occasionally, game theorists examine questions that arise from the work of other game theorists. The most famous example of this is work on the Prisoners' Dilemma. Many scholars have questioned why cooperation did not arise in the Prisoners' Dilemma given that both actors would be better off cooperating than defecting (Axelrod, 1984). As illustrated in Matrix 1.1, both players have an incentive to defect since, regardless of the other player's action, each gains a higher pay-off by defecting.[3] However, mutual defection leaves each player worse off than mutual cooperation.

While the logic of the Prisoners' Dilemma tells us that defection is the equilibrium strategy, many people have noted situations where real world actors seemed to find themselves in situations that resembled the Prisoners' Dilemma and still cooperated. How could this

MATRIX 1.1
A Prisoners' Dilemma

| | | Player 2 | |
		Cooperate	Defect
Player 1	Cooperate	3, 3	1, 4
	Defect	4, 1	2, 2

cooperation arise? This problem is most evident in international relations. In an anarchic world without central authority, why do we see so much cooperation amongst egoistic states? This is the central question that drew Axelrod to this problem.

Axelrod popularized a solution to this problem by considering what would happen when the Prisoners' Dilemma game is iterated. This solution, however, does not work with a game that is iterated a finite number of times and each player is certain of the number of repetitions. In this case, neither player will have an incentive to try to induce cooperation by cooperating themselves. This arises from the fact that there is a known end to the interactions. To illustrate this, let us examine a situation where the Prisoners' Dilemma is repeated three times. Examining the final interaction first, neither player has an incentive to cooperate at this stage because the sole reason to cooperate was to encourage cooperation at a later stage. At the final stage, there is no incentive to encourage further cooperation since it is not possible. As such, each player will defect at this stage. What happens in the second round? In the second round, neither player has an incentive to try to invoke cooperation in the final round since we have already discovered that neither player will cooperate in the final round. As such, both will defect. This same reasoning can be used to show that each player will defect in the first period.[4]

Axelrod found that if the game is repeated an infinite number of times and if each player's discount rate[5] is at a sufficient level, cooperation can arise.[6] This should not be interpreted that repetition always induces cooperation as an equilibrium in a repeated Prisoners' Dilemma. Rather, it is one of the possible equilibria.[7] Moreover, drawing from the results of a series of computer tournaments, Axelrod (1980a, b, 1981, 1984) discussed those strategies most effective in promoting mutual cooperation. He argued that Tit-for-Tat was an especially effective strategy for supporting mutual cooperation. This strategy, which calls for a player to always start cooperating and then mimic the other player's action from the previous round, allows cooperation to evolve and, at the same time, does not encourage players to exploit the cooperative play of another actor. This theoretical solution spawned a sizable literature, especially in international relations, concerning the effect of repetition and reciprocity on cooperation.

Developing Generalizable Predictions

A more common use of game theory is to examine general theoretic questions. For example, a generic problem in the social sciences is how does a leader get his or her followers to follow orders. For example, social psychologists have examined whether leaders are able to work their will because of their charismatic demeanor or because of some trait of their followers. Economists have considered the role of chain stores. Political scientists have written about what makes a president "strong." Scholars of international relations have addressed questions about the role of hegemony.

In this section, we examine this general question from a slightly different perspective. We start with the assumption that a leader can sanction a rebellious follower. However, this sanction imposes costs not only on the follower, but also on the leader. Thus, sanctioning is not costless for the leader, because he would prefer not to sanction wayward followers. If a follower knows this, then she does not have an incentive to cooperate.

How can the leader then induce cooperation? Since undoubtedly this is a repeated interaction, the leader could try to build a reputation for being tough. Possibly, this could be done by the leader punishing rebellious followers early in the process. This would, perhaps, force the followers to "behave" in later stages of the game. This is, of course, the usual notion of how one builds a reputation. However, does it work?

The short answer to this question is, it depends. If the leader and followers believe that there are a finite number of interactions between them, then such an action may not work. Why not? Assume that there will be three interactions between a leader and a given follower. The follower realizes that the leader will not punish any rebellion in the final round because he has no reason to build a reputation and he prefers acquiescing to punishing. What happens in the second round? In the second round, the follower realizes that the leader once again has no incentive to punish a rebellion since the outcome of the final round is already decided. Thus, the follower can rebel without worry of a sanction being imposed by the leader. The same reasoning will lead the follower to decide to rebel in the first period. This logic can be used to show that leaders will never punish if punishment is costly and there is a finite number of interactions. Of course, we are using backward induction in the same manner as noted in the previous section.

How then does a leader get a follower to acquiesce to his demands? Game theorists have offered the following solution to this problem.[8] The follower may not realize what the exact payoffs of the leader are. Instead of punishment being costly, the follower may believe that there is some probability that punishment instead is costless or is even beneficial to the leader. If either of these cases occurs, then a leader may be able to persuade a follower to acquiesce to his demands. In other words, a leader may act tough in the first few rounds of a repeated game in order to persuade his followers to go along with his demands.[9]

The implications from this model have been used to analyze a number of different situations. Calvert (1987) applied this model to the role of leaders in legislative bodies. Alt, Calvert, and Humes (1988) used a similar model of leadership to explain Saudi Arabian actions in keeping OPEC and non-OPEC oil-producing nations in line with formal and informal production quotas. The key to each of these cases is a leader trying to get a follower to acquiesce to his demands. Gates and Hill (1997), using a similar game-theoretic model, showed that even with competition between nonprofit agencies in the delivery of public services, complete control and accountability may still be unattainable.

Examining the Logical Consistency of Arguments

A third and final way to use game theory is to examine the logical consistency of arguments put forward by other scholars. This approach harkens back to Arrow's use of social choice theory in addressing the consistency of "reasonable" properties of rules for aggregating preferences (Arrow, 1951). He showed that a set of widely agreed upon properties for the aggregation of preferences actually is inconsistent.

This approach differs from most approaches of testing theories. Instead of examining questions of external validity, our focus becomes examining internal validity. Thus, we are not testing to see whether the hypotheses derived from a model are supported or rejected by empirical tests. Instead, our focus is on whether the hypotheses are consistent with the theory from which they are derived.

Morrow (1989) used game-theoretic analysis to examine the logical consistency of various empirical models of crisis bargaining and extended deterrence.[10] Morrow accomplished this by developing a game-theoretic model that analyzes how sequence and information orient national actors to select particular actions in a crisis bargaining situation. Morrow uses his formal model "to draw logical links between postulated underlying processes and empirical regularities. By demonstrating what empirical patterns should follow from an assumed process, the formal model serves as a tool to judge evidence" (Morrow, 1989, p. 964).

Morrow's sequential game models the offers and acceptance of offers involved in crisis bargaining. His model demonstrates how selection bias and model misspecification plague empirical models of crisis behavior. Morrow's model demonstrates how a noncrisis is an equilibrium outcome yet empirical models fail to account for noncrisis, thus leading to a selection bias. He also further demonstrated the role of beliefs in determining what actions each side will pursue in a crisis situation. Models that fail to account for the role of beliefs, Morrow argued, are misspecified. By identifying the logical inconsistencies of the empirical literature Morrow was able to correct these problems and draw new conclusions.

Conclusion

In this chapter, we have briefly outlined ways in which game theory can be productively used. These uses are to solve theoretical problems, to develop general implications or predictions, and to examine the logical consistency of theoretical constructs. In the following three chapters, we introduce readers to basic techniques used in game theory. These techniques allow us to use game theory in the manner described above in a variety of disciplines.

2. IMPERFECT AND INCOMPLETE INFORMATION

Chickie Run

Two young men sit across from each other in separate stolen automobiles. They have agreed to settle their difference with a nocturnal "Chickie Run." The two young men are to race their respective cars toward a cliff. The first to jump out wins the ignominious title of "chickie." Of course, waiting too long results in the young man falling, along with car, to a certain death. This, of course, is a version of the game of Chicken from the classic James Dean movie *Rebel Without a Cause*.[11] Most of us are familiar with this version of the game or slightly different ones.[12]

On a more personal level, most of us have experienced a version of this game. How many of us have been confronted by the following situation? You are walking on the right side of the sidewalk and a group that is taking up the whole sidewalk approaches you. What do you do? Do you step to your right, that is, leave the sidewalk open and show your weakness to all, or do you hold your ground, that is, risk the embarrassment of running into a person in the other group? While the end result of the game may not be as catastrophic in this latter example as it was to Buzz in the former example, both share the basic elements of a game of Chicken.

Of course, other situations share similar characteristics with this interaction. For example, various scholars (Schelling, 1966; Snyder, 1971; Snyder and Diesing, 1977; Nicholson, 1989) have argued that mutually assured destruction (MAD) takes on the form of a Chicken game.[13] Other scholars have argued that problems of collective action, which have commonly been modelled as N-person Prisoners' Dilemma games, are more aptly considered as games of Chicken (Taylor, 1976, 1987; Taylor and Ward, 1982). This is especially the case when a certain number of actors out of the total need to contribute to provide the good. For example, defensive alliances may not need to have all potential nations join them to be effective. Instead, they need only a subset of these nations. The problem becomes which subset.[14]

Throughout this book we focus our attention on decisions made by major corporations toward a lobbying effort to affect public policy. Our game is generalized but we start with a particular story. One of the topics addressed by the 1990 Clean Air Act was the issue of gas

8

vapors emitted while pumping gasoline.[15] The major auto companies (we focus in this chapter on two firms, Ford and GM) strongly opposed this measure. They argued that any measure to redesign cars would affect profits. The car companies had two choices: to contribute to a lobbying effort or to not contribute. To simplify the model we assume that both players know how much money it takes to successfully lobby against the policy. Any contribution less than this known amount will be unsuccessful. This means that we assume that lobbying is lumpy rather than continuous (at least in terms of successfully altering policy).

The best outcome for either player is to free-ride when the other corporation contributes an adequate amount to squelch the policy. The second most preferred outcome is when both players contribute to the successful lobbying effort. The third best outcome arises when a player is the sucker (contributing while the other company free-rides). The worst outcome for both would be when neither contributes to the lobbying effort and the policy passes. This ordering of payoffs characterizes the Chicken game. See Matrix 2.1.[16]

Now consider a slightly more complicated version of this game. What if GM did not know exactly the preferences of Ford? Instead, GM knew that Ford could be one of two types: either committed to defeating the policy or uncommitted since Ford had developed a special hood that collected all vapors while filling the tank which could be produced at such negligible cost that lobbying to overturn the policy was not profitable. In order to examine this situation, we need to consider games of incomplete information. These games allow us to consider games in which one or more players is uncertain about the payoffs to the game. The player(s) could be uncertain about other players' payoffs or his (their) own. Before developing examples of incomplete information, we first need to distinguish between perfect information and complete information, but before doing this, we will briefly present the game of Chicken in its normal form.

MATRIX 2.1
A Game of Chicken

| | | Player 2 | |
		Contribute	Not Contribute
Player 1	Contribute	2, 2	1, 4
	Not Contribute	4, 1	0, 0

The Game of Chicken

The normal form of Chicken as presented in Matrix 2.1 is a simple 2×2 two person game with complete and imperfect information. As such, each player has two strategies—not contribute or contribute[17]—known to both players, a set of payoffs known to both players, and no knowledge of what the other player has actually done.[18] Thus, both players possess common knowledge regarding the structure of the game.

This representation of the game captures the essence of the situations described above. Examining things from Player 1's perspective, his most preferred outcome occurs when he chooses to not contribute and the other player contributes. His next preferred outcome arises when both players choose to contribute. This is followed by Player 1 contributing when the second player does not contribute. Of course, the worst outcome for both players is when neither contributes. Since it can be easily seen that this game is symmetric, the payoffs for Player 2 are similar to those of Player 1.

There are three Nash equilibria in this game. A Nash equilibrium is a pair of strategies where neither player is willing to unilaterally change to another strategy. Formally, a Nash equilibrium can be defined as follows. Let s_i represent the ith strategy for Player 1 and t_i represent the ith strategy for Player 2.

Definition 1. A pair of strategies s_i and t_i form a Nash equilibrium iff

$$u_1(s_i|t_i) \geq u_1(s_j|t_i) \; \forall s_i \neq s_j \quad and \quad u_2(t_i|s_i) \geq u_2(t_j|s_i) \; \forall t_i \neq t_j$$

In other words, Player 1's current strategy is his best response to Player 2's strategy, and Player 2's strategy is a best response to Player 1's strategy. The Nash equilibria of this game are (contribute$_1$; not contribute$_2$), (not contribute$_1$; contribute$_2$), and $((\frac{1}{3}$contribute$_1$, $\frac{2}{3}$not contribute$_1$); $(\frac{1}{3}$contribute$_2$, $\frac{2}{3}$not contribute$_2$)).[19] This latter equilibrium is a mixed strategy equilibrium where each player plays contribute with a probability of $\frac{1}{3}$.

While it may be obvious how the pure strategy equilibria were developed, it may not be as obvious how we developed the mixed strategy equilibrium. However, this mystery can be easily addressed. We must first find where Player 1 is indifferent between contribute and not contribute. This is done by setting the expectation of Player 1 playing contribute equal to the expectation of Player 1 playing not contribute (E_1(contribute$_1$) = E_1(not contribute$_1$)). The appropriate calculation where p is the probability that Player 2 chooses contribute is

$$E_1(\text{contribute}_1) = 2p + 1(1 - p)$$
$$E_1(\text{contribute}_1) = 2p + 1 - p$$
$$E_1(\text{contribute}_1) = p + 1$$
$$E_1(\text{not contribute}_1) = 4p + 0(1 - p)$$
$$E_1(\text{not contribute}_1) = 4p$$
$$E_1(\text{contribute}_1) = E_1(\text{not contribute}_1)$$
$$p + 1 = 4p$$
$$1 = 3p$$
$$p = \tfrac{1}{3}$$

Thus, Player 1 will be indifferent between playing contribute and not contribute when Player 2 plays the mixed strategy of $\left(\tfrac{1}{3}\text{contribute}_2, \tfrac{2}{3}\text{not contribute}_2\right)$. Since this is a symmetric game, Player 2 will also be indifferent between playing his two pure strategies when Player 1 chooses the mixed strategy of $\left(\tfrac{1}{3}\text{contribute}_1, \tfrac{2}{3}\text{not contribute}_1\right)$. To see that this is an equilibrium, let us examine the expected payoff of Player 1 given Player 2's mixed strategy. We will examine the expected payoff for Player 1's mixed strategy and then both of Player 1's pure strategies:

$$E_1\left(\tfrac{1}{3}\text{contribute}_1, \tfrac{2}{3}\text{not contribute}_1\right) = \tfrac{1}{3}\left[\tfrac{1}{3}(2) + \tfrac{2}{3}(1)\right]$$
$$+ \tfrac{2}{3}\left[\tfrac{1}{3}(4) + \tfrac{2}{3}(0)\right]$$
$$E_1\left(\tfrac{1}{3}\text{contribute}_1, \tfrac{2}{3}\text{not contribute}_1\right) = \tfrac{4}{9} + \tfrac{8}{9} = \tfrac{12}{9} = \tfrac{4}{3}.$$

Compare this to

$$E_1(\text{not contribute}_1) = \tfrac{1}{3}(4) + \tfrac{2}{3}(0) = \tfrac{4}{3}$$
$$E_1(\text{contribute}_1) = \tfrac{1}{3}(2) + \tfrac{2}{3}(1) = \tfrac{4}{3}$$

Since $E_1\left(\frac{1}{3}\text{contribute}_1, \frac{2}{3}\text{not contribute}_1\right) = E_1(\text{not contribute}_1) = E_1(\text{contribute}_1)$, Player 1 has no incentive to move from this mixed strategy. The reader can easily check that Player 1 will be indifferent between this mixed strategy and any other mixed strategy. As such, this mixed strategy combination is a Nash equilibrium.[20]

We can now move to considering how this basic game may change with changes in the information available to each player. We will first examine the difference between games of perfect and imperfect information. We will then consider complete versus incomplete information.

Games of Perfect and Imperfect Information

The concepts of perfect and imperfect information refer to the information each player has concerning the actions of the other player. A game of imperfect information is one in which neither player knows the actions of the other player before playing her own strategy. For example, Jimmy does not know if Buzz will jump or not jump. Likewise, Buzz does not know if Jimmy will jump or not. Thus, "Chickie Run" is a game of imperfect information. Similarly we see Ford and GM play a Chicken game involving the choices of contribute and not contribute. This game is represented by Matrix 2.1 as well as Figure 2.1, which is the extensive form representation of this game. The dotted line in Figure 2.1 represents that Player 2 does not know what Player 1 has chosen when Player 2 is making his choice. This is known as an information set. This game has the same equilibria, of course, as the game in matrix form.

Consider what happens if Ford knows whether GM has contributed or has not contributed before it has to take an action? Our game is then transformed into the one presented in Figure 2.2. Notice that there are no dotted lines connecting the nodes where Player 2 makes his decision. Player 2 then knows what Player 1 has done when he makes his decision. Of course, this game is not the same one as presented in Matrix 2.1. The proper normal form representation is given in Matrix 2.2.

This game has three pure strategy Nash equilibria. The set of pure strategy equilibria has expanded because the strategy space for Player 2 has also expanded. For this player, each strategy must take into account how the player will react to each of Player 1's potential strategies. Thus, Player 2's strategies each have two parts. Each part

12

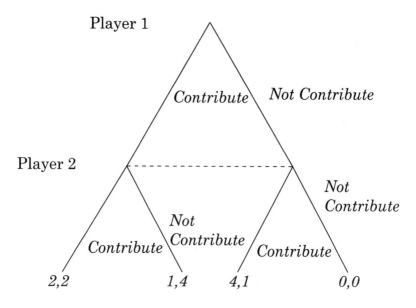

Player 1

Contribute   Not Contribute

Player 2

Not
Contribute

Contribute   Not
Contribute   Contribute

2,2   1,4   4,1   0,0

Figure 2.1. An Extensive Form Game of Chicken With Imperfect Information

is conditional on Player 1's action. For example, examine Player 2's strategy (contribute$_2$, not contribute$_2$). This strategy calls for Player 2 to play contribute if Player 1 plays contribute and to play not contribute if Player 1 plays not contribute. The three pure strategy Nash equilibria are (contribute$_1$; (not contribute$_2$, not contribute$_2$)), (not contribute$_1$; (contribute$_2$, contribute$_2$)), and (not contribute$_1$; (not contribute$_2$, contribute$_2$)).[21]

Changing the game from a game of perfect information to a game of imperfect information results in a change in the equilibria of the game. How can we choose between these different equilibria? In order to do so, we must use a refinement of the Nash equilibrium concept. One such refinement is a subgame perfect equilibrium. The purpose of this and other refinements is to allow us to choose between different Nash equilibria. For an equilibrium to be subgame perfect, it must result from each player making rational moves in each subgame of the game. Formally, a subgame perfect equilibrium can be defined as follows.

Player 1

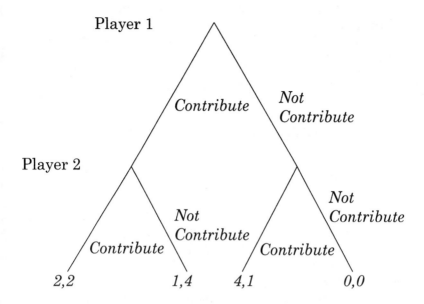

Figure 2.2. An Extensive Form Game of Chicken With Perfect Information

Definition 2. A set of strategies is subgame perfect if for every subgame, the restriction of those strategies to the subgames forms a Nash equilibrium (Morrow, 1994, p. 129).

In order to illustrate this concept, we will examine each of the equilibria in turn to see if they satisfy these conditions. Taking the equilibria in the order mentioned above, we first examine (contribute$_1$; (not contribute$_2$, not contribute$_2$)). Not contribute is the rational move in the first subgame for Player 2 since he receives a payoff of 4 instead of 2. However, in the second subgame, Player

MATRIX 2.2
A Game of Chicken with Perfect Information

		Player 2			
		Contribute, Contribute	Contribute, Not Contribute	Not Contribute, Contribute	Not Contribute, Not Contribute
Player 1	Contribute	2, 2	2, 2	1, 4	1, 4
	Not Contribute	4, 1	0, 0	4, 1	0, 0

2 should choose contribute instead of not contribute because he would receive a payoff of 1 instead of 0. Thus, this equilibrium is not subgame perfect.

This Nash equilibrium illustrates the reason for this refinement. The only reason it is a Nash equilibrium is because Player 2 has lodged a noncredible threat. He has announced that he will play not contribute in the second subgame despite the fact that he would be better off playing contribute if this subgame was ever reached.

The second Nash equilibrium reported above, (not contribute$_1$; (contribute$_2$, contribute$_2$)) is also not subgame perfect. In this case, Player 2 has chosen to play contribute in the first subgame instead of not contribute. However, the latter strategy would yield him a payoff of 4 instead of the former's payoff of 2. Unlike the previous Nash equilibrium, this one does not result from a noncredible threat. In fact, if Player 2 changes his action from contribute to not contribute in the first subgame, we are left with the final Nash equilibrium (not contribute$_1$; (not contribute$_2$, contribute$_2$)), which is subgame perfect. As argued previously, the optimal response by Player 2 in the first subgame is not contribute since he prefers 4 to 2. Likewise, Player 2's optimal response in the second subgame is contribute since 4 is greater than 0. This is the only subgame perfect equilibrium in this game.

What if the game were slightly different? A game of one-sided chicken is presented in Matrix 2.3. Player 2 has the same preferences as in Matrix 2.1. Player 1, however, now has a dominant strategy. A dominant strategy is one where the player receives her best payoffs regardless of the strategy of the other player. Formally, a dominant strategy can be defined as follows.

Definition 3. A strategy s_i is a dominant strategy iff $u_1(s_i|t_i) \geq u_1(s_j|t_i) \ \forall s_i \neq s_j$ and $\forall t_i$.

MATRIX 2.3
A Game of One-Sided Chicken

		Player 2	
		Contribute	Not Contribute
Player 1	Contribute	1, 2	0, 4
	Not Contribute	4, 1	2, 0

15

For Player 1, the dominant strategy not contribute yields a better payoff than contribute regardless of the action of Player 2. As such, there is only one Nash equilibrium in this game: (not contribute₁; contribute₂).

Figure 2.3 represents where the game preceding has been transformed into a game of perfect information. There are only two Nash equilibria in this game: (not contribute₁; (contribute₂, contribute₂)) and (not contribute₁; (not contribute₂, contribute₂)). Only the former of these is a subgame perfect equilibrium.

What if the order in which the players move is changed? Figure 2.4 and Matrix 2.4 present our original game of Chicken with perfect information.[22] However, here we have Player 2 moving first. As you might expect, since this form of Chicken is symmetric, the equilibria of this game are similar to those of our original game. These equilibria are ((contribute₁, contribute₁); not contribute₂), ((not contribute₁, contribute₁); not contribute₂), and ((not contribute₁, not contribute₁); contribute₂)[23]. Only the middle set of these Nash

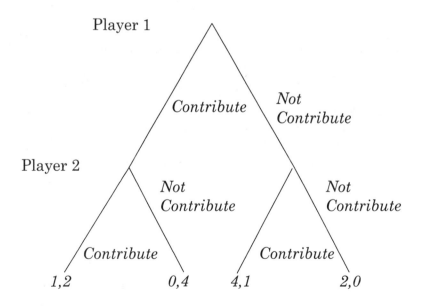

Figure 2.3. An Extensive Form Game of One-Sided Chicken With Perfect Information

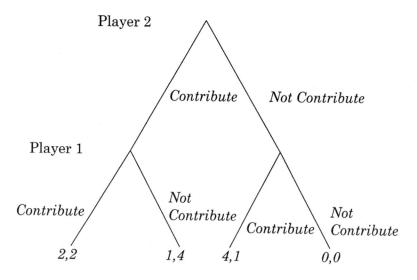

Figure 2.4. A Revised Version of an Extensive Form Game of Chicken With Perfect Information

equilibria is subgame perfect. Of course, while the number of Nash equilibria stay the same, changing the order of the game has an effect on what these equilibria look like. For example, examine the subgame perfect equilibrium of this game. The strategy pair $((\text{not contribute}_1, \text{contribute}_1); \text{not contribute}_2)$, is more advantageous to Player 2 than the subgame perfect equilibrium of the original game which was $(\text{not contribute}_1; (\text{not contribute}_2, \text{contribute}_2))$. Thus, while the number of Nash equilibria and subgame perfect equi-

MATRIX 2.4

A Revised Version of a Game of Chicken with Perfect Information

			Player 2	
			Contribute	Not Contribute
	Contribute,	Contribute	2, 2	1, 4
Player 1	Contribute,	Not Contribute	2, 2	0, 0
	Not Contribute,	Contribute	4, 1	1, 1
	Not Contribute,	Not Contribute	4, 1	0, 0

MATRIX 2.5

A Revised Version of a One-Sided Game of Chicken with
Perfect Information

			Player 2	
			Contribute	Not Contribute
Player 1	Contribute,	Contribute	1, 2	0, 4
	Contribute,	Not Contribute	1, 2	2, 0
	Not Contribute,	Contribute	4, 1	0, 4
	Not Contribute,	Not Contribute	4, 1	2, 0

libria do not change, the order of moves does make a difference to the two players.

Matrix 2.5 provides the representation of our one-sided game of Chicken with perfect information where Player 2 moves first. Here the order of moves once again does make a difference. Unlike the previous perfect information game, this game only has one Nash equilibrium: ((not contribute$_1$, not contribute$_1$); contribute$_2$). This equilibrium is subgame perfect and is similar to the subgame perfect equilibrium of our earlier version of this game. Thus, order has allowed us to eliminate one of the Nash equilibria from the previous version of one-sided Chicken.

In this section, we have developed the concepts of perfect and imperfect information. In addition, we have introduced the concept of subgame perfect equilibrium. We have also shown how order can matter in games of perfect information. In the next section, we examine a different informational concern when we examine the difference between complete and incomplete information.

Games of Complete and Incomplete Information

Besides focusing on whether a player is aware of the previous actions of other players, there is another type of information with which we need to be concerned. The games considered previously all assumed that each player knew the payoffs of the other player. What if this were not the case? For example, what if Ford did not know exactly the preferences of GM? Maybe Ford had heard rumors that alluded to GM having developed a cheap mechanism to deal with gasoline fumes. Is GM committed to fight the policy through lobbying or not? Ford may not be able to decide which type of player it is facing and, hence, which game it is playing.

If Ford attaches probabilities to these preferences and GM knows what these probabilities or beliefs are, then we can use game theory to examine this strategic situation. Harsanyi (1967), in a series of articles, first presented a way in which to analyze games of incomplete information. A game of complete information is one in which both players are aware of each other's payoffs. As such, a game of incomplete information is one in which one or both of the players do not know the payoffs of the other. If only one player lacks this information, the game is referred to as a game of one-sided incomplete information. If both players lack such information, then it is referred to as a game of two-sided incomplete information.

Figure 2.5 represents the uncertainty that Ford, our Player 1, faces when playing this game with GM, our Player 2. This game starts with Nature making a choice between playing Type I or Type II. It does so with probabilities α and $1 - \alpha$, respectively. A Type I choice leads to our original game of Chicken, while a choice of Type II leads to a game of one-sided Chicken. Both of these choices by Nature lead to games of perfect information. After Nature chooses Player 1's type, Player 1 chooses whether to contribute or not contribute. Player 1 is aware of his type when he makes this decision. Player 2 then chooses to contribute or not contribute. Player 2 is aware of Player 1's action; however, he does not know the type of Player 1. The reader should be able to see this situation with the manner in which the information sets operate in this game. The information set indicates Player 1's actions but not his/her type. Another perspective is that he does not know which game he is playing. Is he playing a game of Chicken or a game of one-sided Chicken?

Player 2 may be able to learn something about Player 1's type by examining his action—contribute or not contribute—as well as his strategy while taking into consideration his beliefs about what type of player he is facing. Since Player 2 will be examining not only Player 1's choice of strategies but also his own beliefs about Player 1's type, we will need to change our notion of equilibria somewhat. Instead of searching for Nash equilibria, we will use the concept of perfect Bayesian equilibria. A perfect Bayesian equilibrium is a combination of strategies such that neither player prefers to unilaterally change strategies with the addition that their decisions are informed by Player

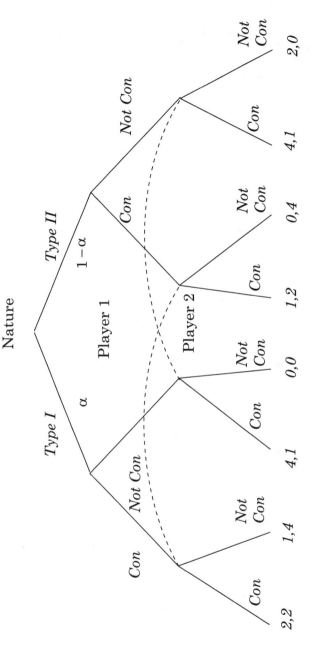

Figure 2.5. A Game of Incomplete Information Combining a Game of Chicken and a Game of One-Sided Chicken (Con = Contribute; Not Con = Not Contribute)

2's beliefs concerning whether Player 1 is a Type I or a Type II player. Formally, a perfect Bayesian equilibrium can be defined as follows.

Definition 4. A perfect Bayesian equilibrium is a strategy combination $(s_i; t_i)$ and a set of beliefs μ such that for each node of the game (1) the strategies for the remainder of the game are Nash given the beliefs and strategies of the other players; (2) the beliefs at each information set are rational given the evidence appearing that far in the game (meaning that they are based, if possible, on priors updated by Bayes' rule given the observed actions of the other players under the hypothesis that they are in equilibrium; Rasmusen, 1989, p, 110).

In order to better understand this concept, let us examine a potential strategy combination.

Player 1:   If Type I, then choose not contribute.
            If Type II, then choose not contribute.
Player 2:   If Player 1 chooses contribute, then choose not contribute.
            If Player 1 chooses not contribute, then choose contribute.

We will now examine this strategy combination in order to see whether any set of beliefs supports it as an equilibrium. We do so by using Bayes' rule:

$$P(\text{Type I}|\text{not contribute}_1)$$

$$= \frac{P(\text{not contribute}_1|\text{Type I})P(\text{Type I})}{[P(\text{not contribute}_1|\text{Type I})P(\text{Type I}) + P(\text{not contribute}_1|\text{Type II})P(\text{Type II})]}$$

This yields

$$P(\text{Type I}|\text{not contribute}_1) = \frac{1\alpha}{1\alpha + (1-\alpha)1} = \alpha$$

The reader should note that Player 2 does not gather any new information by observing Player 1's action of not contribute. His prior estimate of the probability that Player 1 is a Type I player, α, is the same as his updated probability. Of course, this should not be a surprise since Player 1's strategy calls for him to choose not contribute regardless of his type.

Given this probability, how should Player 2 react to a choice of not contribute by Player 1? In order to evaluate this choice, we will examine the expected values of playing contribute versus not contribute. These expectations are calculated as

$$E_2(\text{contribute}_2|\text{not contribute}_1) = \alpha 1 + (1 - \alpha)1 = 1$$
$$E_2(\text{not contribute}_2|\text{not contribute}_1) = \alpha 0 + (1 - \alpha)0 = 0$$

This yields that $E_2(\text{contribute}_2|\text{not contribute}_1)$ is always greater than $E_2(\text{not contribute}_2|\text{not contribute}_1)$ for all values of α. As such, Player 2 will not unilaterally change his strategy from contribute to not contribute when he observes Player 1 playing not contribute. One can easily see that Player 2 will not change the first part of his strategy either because he is always strictly better off if he plays not contribute when Player 1 plays contribute. Also, this part of his strategy will never be reached since Player 1 always chooses not contribute.

In order for there to be an equilibrium, Player 1 should also prefer not to unilaterally change his strategy given the strategy of Player 2. It should also be obvious that Player 1 has no incentive to change his strategy because he can always do better by playing not contribute given Player 2's strategy. Thus, a perfect Bayesian equilibrium of this game is as follows.

Player 1:   If Type I, then choose not contribute.
            If Type II, then choose not contribute.
Player 2:   If Player 1 chooses contribute, then choose not contribute.
            If Player 1 chooses not contribute, then choose contribute
            $\forall \alpha$.

This equilibrium is sometimes referred to as a pooling equilibrium. It is called a pooling equilibrium because Player 1 chooses the same strategy regardless of his type. Thus, Player 2 cannot learn anything from observing Player 1's action. If, in equilibrium, Player 1 would instead choose different strategies depending on his type, then we would have a separating equilibrium.

Are there any other perfect Bayesian equilibria in this game? To answer this question, we need to examine all the different combinations of strategies for each player. If we limit ourselves to pure strategies, then there are 16 cases to consider. Of the 15 remaining cases,[24] we can easily eliminate 8 of the cases that contain Player 1 choosing contribute if he is a Type II player. Player 1 is always better off playing not contribute in this situation since he has a dominant strategy in the one-sided Chicken game. Thus, we have seven strategy combinations remaining to examine.

We will first examine a strategy combination that is very similar to the one developed in our original example:

Player 1: If Type I, then choose not contribute.
    If Type II, then choose not contribute.
Player 2: If Player 1 chooses contribute, then choose not contribute.
    If Player 1 chooses not contribute, then choose not contribute.

This combination is not a perfect Bayesian equilibrium regardless of the beliefs of the two players because we have showed previously that $E_2(\text{contribute}_2 | \text{not contribute}_1) > E_2(\text{not contribute}_2 | \text{not contribute}_1)$ for all values of α. As such, Player 2 will change "If Player 1 chooses not contribute, then choose not contribute" to "If Player 1 chooses not contribute, then choose contribute." This same reasoning can be used to eliminate the following strategy as an equilibrium.

Player 1: If Type I, then choose not contribute.
    If Type II, then choose not contribute.
Player 2: If Player 1 chooses contribute, then choose contribute.
    If Player 1 chooses not contribute, then choose not contribute.

Tweaking these strategies again, we present the following strategy combination.

Player 1: If Type I, then choose not contribute.
    If Type II, then choose not contribute.
Player 2: If Player 1 chooses contribute, then choose contribute.
    If Player 1 chooses not contribute, then choose contribute.

Is this another pooling equilibrium? To answer this question, we compare this strategy to our earlier pooling equilibrium. The only difference in this strategy is that Player 2 chooses contribute when Player 1 chooses contribute. Since Player 1 will never choose contribute, this difference does not have any actual affect on the actions of the players. However, it is not a perfect Bayesian equilibrium since Player 2 is not behaving rationally off the equilibrium path. For it to be a perfect Bayesian equilibrium, Player 2's strategy must call for him to choose the rational alternative regardless of whether that action is ever called for.[25] It should be obvious to the reader that Player 2 should always choose not contribute if Player 1 has chosen contribute.

There are four other pure strategy combinations to explore. These all call for Player 1 to choose contribute if he is Type I and to choose not contribute if he is Type 2. The first such combination is as follows.

Player 1: If Type I, then choose contribute.
          If Type II, then choose not contribute.
Player 2: If Player 1 chooses contribute, then choose not contribute.
          If Player 1 chooses not contribute, then choose not contribute.

This strategy combination is not part of a perfect Bayesian equilibrium since Player 2 can unilaterally make himself better off by choosing to reply to not contribute with contribute. This reasoning also eliminates the following strategy combination from consideration.

Player 1: If Type I, then choose contribute.
          If Type II, then choose not contribute.
Player 2: If Player 1 chooses contribute, then choose contribute.
          If Player 1 chooses not contribute, then choose not contribute.

We now explore the following strategy combination. This strategy combination is eliminated from consideration since player 2 can always make himself better off by responding to contribute with not contribute instead of contribute.

Player 1: If Type I, then choose contribute.
          If Type II, then choose not contribute.
Player 2: If Player 1 chooses contribute, then choose contribute.
          If Player 1 chooses not contribute, then choose contribute.

The final combination to explore is given subsequently. This combination is not part of a perfect Bayesian equilibrium since Player 1 would always be better off by changing "If Type I, then choose contribute" to "If Type I, then choose not contribute." This is because of Player 2's strategy. Player 2 reacts to not contribute with contribute. As such, Player 1 would be better off playing not contribute regardless of his type. Thus, we can eliminate this combination.

Player 1:   If Type I, then choose contribute.
            If Type II, then choose not contribute.
Player 2:   If Player 1 chooses contribute, then choose not contribute.
            If Player 1 chooses not contribute, then choose contribute.

While we have examined all the pure strategy cases, we have not examined any cases involving mixed strategies. Below we examine two cases in order to illustrate how such cases are examined. The first strategy combination to be examined has Player 1 playing a mixed strategy when she is a Type I player and a pure strategy when she is a Type II player.[26] This strategy is as follows.

Player 1:   If Type I, then choose $\left(\frac{1}{3}\text{contribute}, \frac{2}{3}\text{not contribute}\right)$.[27]
            If Type II, then choose not contribute.
Player 2:   If contribute, then not contribute.
            If not contribute, then contribute.

We must first calculate

$$P(\text{Type I}|\text{not contribute}_1)$$

$$= \frac{P(\text{not contribute}_1|\text{Type I})P(\text{Type I})}{[P(\text{not contribute}_1|\text{Type I})P(\text{Type I}) + P(\text{not contribute}_1|\text{Type II})P(\text{Type II})]}$$

$$P(\text{Type I}|\text{not contribute}_1) = \frac{\frac{2}{3}\alpha}{\frac{2}{3}\alpha + 1(1-\alpha)}$$

$$P(\text{Type I}|\text{not contribute}_1) = \frac{\frac{2}{3}\alpha}{1 - \frac{1}{3}\alpha}$$

The $P(\text{Type II}|\text{not contribute}_1)$ then is

$$P(\text{Type I}|\text{not contribute}_1) = \frac{1-\alpha}{1 - \frac{1}{3}\alpha}$$

We now use these probabilities to examine whether Player 2 will change the last part of his strategy. This is done by comparing the $E_2(\text{contribute}_2|\text{not contribute}_1)$ and the $E_2(\text{not contribute}_2|\text{not contribute}_1)$ expectations:

$$E_2(\text{contribute}_2|\text{not contribute}_1)$$

$$= 1\left(\frac{\frac{2}{3}\alpha}{1 - \frac{1}{3}\alpha}\right) + 1\left(\frac{1 - \alpha}{1 - \frac{1}{3}\alpha}\right) = 1$$

and

$$E_2(\text{not contribute}_2|\text{not contribute}_1)$$

$$= 0\left(\frac{\frac{2}{3}\alpha}{1 - \frac{1}{3}\alpha}\right) + 0\left(\frac{1 - \alpha}{1 - \frac{1}{3}\alpha}\right) = 0$$

Thus, the $E_2(\text{contribute}_2|\text{not contribute}_1)$ will always be greater than the $E_2(\text{not contribute}_2|\text{not contribute}_1)$. We next need to examine whether Player 2 will change the first part of his strategy. In order to do this we need to calculate the $P(\text{Type II}|\text{contribute}_1)$ and then use this probability to calculate the $E_2(\text{contribute}_2|\text{contribute}_1)$ and the $E_2(\text{not contribute}_2|\text{contribute}_1)$:

$$P(\text{Type II}|\text{contribute}_1)$$

$$= \frac{P(\text{contribute}_1|\text{Type II})P(\text{Type II})}{[P(\text{contribute}_1|\text{Type II})P(\text{Type II}) + P(\text{contribute}_1|\text{Type I})P(\text{Type I})]}$$

$$P(\text{Type II}|\text{contribute}_1) = \frac{0(1 - \alpha)}{0(1 - \alpha) + \frac{1}{3}\alpha} = 0$$

The $P(\text{Type I}|\text{contribute}_1)$ then is 1. The resulting expectations then are

$$E_2(\text{not contribute}_2|\text{contribute}_1) = 4(1) + 4(0) = 4$$

and

$$E_2(\text{contribute}_2|\text{contribute}_1) = 2(1) + 2(0) = 2$$

Thus, once again Player 2 does not have an incentive to unilaterally change his strategy given that he expects to receive more from responding to contribute with a not contribute than with a contribute.

Of course for this strategy combination to be an equilibrium, we also must examine the strategy choice of Player 1. Specifically, we need to check whether this player would be willing to move from her mixed strategy to a pure strategy. To do so, we must examine her expected payoffs of playing the mixed strategy as well as playing the possible pure strategies. These expectations are

$$E_1\left(\tfrac{1}{3}\text{contribute}, \tfrac{2}{3}\text{not contribute}\right) = \tfrac{1}{3}(1) + \tfrac{2}{3}(4) = 3$$

$$E_1(\text{not contribute}) = 4$$

Given that $E_1(\text{not contribute})$ is greater than $E_1\left(\tfrac{1}{3}\text{contribute}, \tfrac{2}{3}\text{not contribute}\right)$, the preceding strategy combination cannot be an equilibrium since Player 1 has an incentive to change her strategy if she is a Type I player. This change occurs, of course, because of the way Player 2 reacts to player 1 choosing to not contribute. What if we changed this part of Player 2's strategy? Would this change result in a mixed strategy equilibrium? We examine this strategy combination:

Player 1:   If Type I, then choose $\left(\tfrac{1}{3}\text{contribute}, \tfrac{2}{3}\text{not contribute}\right)$.

           If Type II, then choose not contribute.

Player 2:   If contribute, then $\left(\tfrac{1}{3}\text{contribute}, \tfrac{2}{3}\text{not contribute}\right)$.

           If not contribute, then $\left(\tfrac{1}{3}\text{contribute}, \tfrac{2}{3}\text{not contribute}\right)$.

We can show that this is not an equilibrium by showing that the expectation of Player 2 playing a mixed strategy given that Player 1 has played contribute is less than the utility Player 2 gets from playing not contribute given that Player 1 played contribute. Given that we can use the probabilities developed in the previous case here, the above-mentioned expected value is equal to

$$E_2\left(\tfrac{1}{3}\text{contribute}_2, \tfrac{2}{3}\text{not contribute}_2 | \text{contribute}_1\right)$$
$$= \tfrac{1}{3}\big[u_2(\text{contribute}_2 | \text{Type I}, \text{contribute}_1)P(\text{Type I}|\text{contribute}_1)$$
$$+ u_2(\text{contribute}_2 | \text{Type II}, \text{contribute}_1)$$
$$\times P(\text{Type II}|\text{contribute}_1)\big]$$

$$+ \tfrac{2}{3}[u_2(\text{not contribute}_2|\text{Type I, contribute}_1)$$
$$\times \text{P(Type I}|\text{contribute}_1)$$
$$+ u_2(\text{not contribute}_2|\text{Type II, contribute}_1)$$
$$\times \text{P(Type II}|\text{contribute}_1)]$$
$$E_2\big(\tfrac{1}{3}\text{contribute}_2, \tfrac{2}{3}\text{not contribute}_2|\text{contribute}_1\big)$$
$$= \tfrac{1}{3}[2(1) + 1(0)] + \tfrac{2}{3}[4(1) + 4(0)] = \tfrac{11}{3}$$

This value is, of course, less than $E_2(\text{not contribute}_2|\text{contribute}_1)$, which from previous statement is equal to 4. Thus, this strategy combination cannot be an equilibrium since Player 2 would want to switch from his mixed strategy to a pure strategy in the situation where Player 2 chose contribute.

Thus, this modified game of Chicken has only one equilibrium. This equilibrium calls for Player 1 to not contribute regardless of his type and Player 2 to react to this strategy by choosing contribute. Thus, GM would choose not contribute and Ford would contribute. This is not what happened in 1971 with the Clean Air Act, when both automobile companies lobbied and passed the costs of dealing with gasoline fumes on to the service stations. On the other hand, the outcome presented here is equivalent to not jump and jump. This is, of course, what occurred in the movie *Rebel Without a Cause*.

Generalized Payoffs

Assigning payoffs of cardinal values is most certainly a big simplification of the game played between Ford and GM. In this section we present the game with more generalized payoffs and then identify the Nash equilibria for the incomplete information version of this game. The advantage of using more generalized payoffs is that we are not limiting our study to a very small set of payoffs.

We focus here on three parameters. First we consider profits gained by successfully lobbying against the Clean Air Act, which are designated P. Second are lobby costs, L. Finally we consider the market share that is lost by being identified by the public to be against clean air (R). As we noted previously, the best outcome for either player is to free-ride, whereby the other corporation contributes an adequate amount of money to lobbying to squelch the policy. Consider Ford to be the free-rider. In this situation, GM derives the benefits of P from successfully lobbying against the policy. However, GM must subtract from these profits the cost of lobbying, L. Moreover, by lobbying against the Clean Air Act, GM is identified by a set of the public as a "bad" company and GM loses a market share, R. Ford, on the other hand, earns the profits, P, from GM's lobbying efforts and gains the market share, R, from GM. GM then earns a payoff of $P - L - R$ and Ford gets $P + R$. These payoffs are reversed if GM free-rides. If both sides contribute, both firms receive the payoff of $P - L$, and since both firms fight against the policy, there is no transfer of market share, R. If neither firm contributes to lobbying, then they both receive nothing since there are no profits, no market share is lost, and there are no lobbying costs. These payoffs satisfy the inequalities $P + R > P - L > P - L - R > 0$. This game is presented in Matrix 2.6. Given these payoffs, the generalized equilibria for this game are (contribute$_1$; not contribute$_2$), (not contribute$_1$; contribute$_2$), and a mixed strategy equilibrium which takes the form

$$\left(\left(\frac{P - L - R}{P} \text{contribute}_1, \frac{L + R}{P} \text{not contribute}_1 \right);$$
$$\left(\frac{P - L - R}{P} \text{contribute}_2, \frac{L + R}{P} \text{not contribute}_2 \right) \right).^{28}$$

We can also generalize the game of incomplete information developed in the previous section. This game is illustrated in Figure 2.6. For illustrative purposes, we examine the first set of strategies presented with the original game:

Player 1:   If Type I, then choose not contribute.
              If Type II, then choose not contribute.

MATRIX 2.6
A Generalized Game of Chicken

		GM	
		Contribute	Not Contribute
Ford	Contribute	$P - L, P - L$	$P - L - R, P + R$
	Not Contribute	$P + R, P - L - R$	$0, 0$

$P + R > P - L > P - L - R > 0$

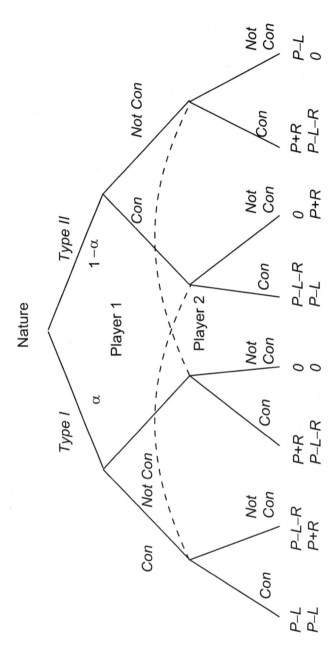

Figure 2.6. A Game of Incomplete Information Combining a Game of Chicken and a Game of One-Sided Chicken (Con = Contribute; Not Con = Not Contribute)

29

Player 2: If Player 1 chooses contribute, then choose not contribute.
   If Player 1 chooses not contribute, then choose contribute.

From our previous discussion, we found that the $P(\text{Type I}|\text{contribute}_1) = \alpha$ and the probability of $P(\text{Type II}|\text{not contribute}_1) = 1 - \alpha$. Using this information, we develop the following expectations:

$$E_2(\text{contribute}_2|\text{not contribute}_1) = \alpha(P - L - R) + (1 - \alpha)(P + R)$$
$$E_2(\text{contribute}_2|\text{not contribute}_1) = P - \alpha L + R - 2\alpha R$$

and

$$E_2(\text{not contribute}_2|\text{not contribute}_1) = \alpha(0) + (1 - \alpha)(0)$$
$$E_2(\text{not contribute}_2|\text{not contribute}_1) = 0$$

Using these expectations, we now examine the inequality

$$E_2(\text{contribute}_2|\text{not contribute}_1)$$
$$> E_2(\text{not contribute}_2|\text{not contribute}_1)$$
$$P - \alpha L + R - 2\alpha R > 0$$
$$- \alpha L - 2\alpha R > -P - R$$
$$\alpha L + 2\alpha R < P + R$$
$$\alpha < \frac{P + R}{L + 2R}$$

Thus, this is a perfect Bayesian equilibrium if the inequality holds. Our next question should be under what conditions does this inequality hold. Since we know from before that $P - L - R > 0$, it is elementary to show that $P + R > L + 2R$. Thus, the foregoing strategy combination is an equilibrium for all possible values of α since the quantity on the right-hand side of the inequality will always be greater than 1 and α, by definition, is bounded between 0 and 1.

We will not examine the other possible strategy combinations in this game because of space limitations. However, the reader should note that some games possess perfect Bayesian equilibria that are supported by certain α's or beliefs which are some proper subset of the interval between 0 and 1. In these cases, the value of α plays more of a role than it does here.

Conclusion

In this chapter, we introduced the concepts of perfect information, imperfect information, complete information, incomplete information, Nash equilibrium, subgame perfect equilibrium, and perfect Bayesian equilibrium. Besides introducing these concepts, we have shown how we can analyze games of incomplete information. This allows us to analyze games in which a player is uncertain about one or more other players' payoffs.

3. REPEATED GAMES

Honor Without End

It's late at night two weeks later. Both Buzz and Jimmy's stolen cars have been "Bondoed" and repaired on a nightly basis. The police are amazingly ignorant of the location of the stolen vehicles. Buzz and Jimmy, having taken their share of falls, limp toward their cars for yet another night of the Chickie Run. Susie, playing the sexist male's image of a girl without any options or actions of her own, prepares to wave her arms bravely for yet another night. Will Buzz jump? Will Jimmy jump? Who will Susie love? Will Susie get in her own car and run them both over?[29] Suppose that Buzz (or Jimmy) can survive the fall over the cliff. They meet nightly to once again prove themselves to their peers and to each other. Have they acquired new information about each other from the preceding two weeks that they can use to stop the punishing beating they, their cars, or their honor are taking? Should they have updated their beliefs about the expected actions of the other person previously?

Most of us intuitively believe that we should be able to update our beliefs about others from our past interactions with people with whom we are engaged in ongoing relationships. We would like to think that Buzz and Jimmy would choose their actions in their nightly display of testosterone-driven honor based on their expectation of what the other may choose and knowledge of what the other chose last time. We would wonder whether they had explored creating a mutually cooperative relationship where each could benefit. There are many situations where humans are engaged in ongoing repeated interactions with another person. The concept of repeated games in game theory helps us to think about the kinds of patterns of actions that may occur in repeated interactions with another.

GM and Ford certainly maintain an ongoing relationship. These two giant auto producers regularly must make decisions whether or not to support lobbying efforts to alter public policy that affects them. Such a game can be generalized in the form described in Chapter 2. Nonetheless, each round of the game can hardly be considered in isolation. Both Ford and GM will take into account previous actions taken by the other. How does a repeated game played between the two auto giants differ from the single round of the game?

As in the previous chapter, we are especially interested in patterns of behavior that are in equilibrium, thus implying that they are the best that each person can accomplish unilaterally given the information available and the choices made by the other person. When analyzing repeated interactions, we often are looking for the development of reciprocity or cooperation to see if it is a stable strategy. However, these normative-laden terms do not characterize the only potential stable strategies. It may be that the best a person can do in a repeated interaction is to minimize his/her losses. Certainly, we know that everyone is trying to maximize what he/she can personally derive from the relationship. The concept of a repeated game allows for persons to choose at any stage of an interaction contingent on the previous choices of the other person. Contingent choice based on the history of the repeated game is the focus of repeated games.

Definitions and Different Types of Repetition

Whereas repeated games explore how two persons may or may not develop a contingent "understanding" solely on the basis of previous interactions, we need to develop several concepts. We first need to consider what we mean by a repeated game. A repeated game is a series of constituent or stage games. In the case of GM and Ford hypothesized previously, the game could consist of a series of nightly meetings, which would create a repeated game of Chicken. Any particular night would be a stage in the game. Payoffs are awarded at the end of each stage game, $n = 1, 2, 3, \ldots$, and summed for a total payoff for the repeated game.

A strategy would be the series of choices for each stage, as if each player chose in advance what to do on a night by night basis. Each player can choose to do more than always contribute, always not contribute, or alternate on some basis. They can make plans contingent on the history of the other player. In the foregoing scenario, Ford could have set a strategy on the 14th year of play based on all 13 of GM's previous decisions, the last two decisions, or even the last, most recent decision by GM. This idea comes from the fact that each of us wants to know whether to hold long or short memories or grudges by which we reward or punish people in our repeated interactions. The length of the history of previous moves that one might want to use may be a function of the payoffs of the stage game and the discount we apply in our minds to future interactions. As such, the concept of a strategy becomes more complicated because it must represent the *contingent* choice, if any, for every stage of the game.

The final concept we need to introduce is discounting. Discounting refers to how a player values a payoff in the present versus the same payoff in the future. We assume that the discount rate is less than 1. This results in each player valuing a payoff of x greater in the current period than in the future.

We will first look at strategies in the repeated games where the set of interactions is finite and known. Second, we will develop repeated games when the interaction is infinite. Third, we will look at what happens when the interaction is finite but with a probability of when the game will stop, such as when GM goes bankrupt.[30]

Finite Repeated Games: The Role of Backward Induction

By looking first at the finite game, we can better understand the complexity of strategies in a repeated game and how strategies may become contingent on previous actions and outcomes. A stage game consists of the single-shot game of interest, Z, played once. The strategies chosen within each stage game we will call actions so as not to confuse the strategies of the repeated game with what takes place inside each stage game. The entire game, Z^n, consists of the series of n stage games of Z.[31] The series of actions taken in each stage game by both players will be called a strategy profile, which is distinct from the idea of an overarching strategy in that it represents the actual moves of each player for each stage game. The summation of the payoffs from the stage games provides the total payoff for the game.[32] Formally, the total payoff for Player 1 is, $\sum_{t=0}^{t=n} X_t$, where X_t is the payoff to Player 1 for the stage game at time t.

We will limit our exploration for the purposes of clarity to a three stage-game interaction. When examining finite repeated games, it is important to use backward induction to check for subgame perfect strategies. Backward induction helps to check for the likelihood of reneging on stage-game strategies that might otherwise develop through tacit reciprocity.

Backward induction involves examining what players would do at the last stage of the game, then using this information to examine what the players would do at the penultimate stage, and continuing this process until we finally consider the first stage of the repeated game. Backward induction is perhaps most well known from the Prisoners'

MATRIX 3.1

A Prisoners' Dilemma

		Player 2	
		Cooperate	*Defect*
Player 1	*Cooperate*	3, 3	1, 4
	Defect	4, 1	2, 2

Dilemma framework. In a Prisoners' Dilemma game as represented in Matrix 3.1, both players in any stage game have an incentive to defect as a function of their mutual dominant strategies. In a repeated game of Prisoners' Dilemma, we want to know if both players could tacitly collude to cooperate at each stage, thus enjoying the stream of higher payoffs, $(3, 3)$, from mutual cooperation than the lower pair $(2, 2)$ resulting from mutual defection.

With a finite number of repetitions, each player knows that the other could benefit in the final stage game of the repeated game by defecting from a stream of cooperative choices. Player 1 knows that Player 2 will see her incentive to defect in the final stage game. As such, Player 1 also will defect in that final stage game. Then in the penultimate stage game, Player 1 knows that Player 2 will also have an incentive to defect in the penultimate game as it is well expected that the last stage game will yield a defection. In order to protect herself again, Player 1 will also defect in the penultimate, or in this case, the second stage game. Finally, then, in the first stage game, both players know that each has the incentive to defect since every game following has defections built backward from the logic of the final stage game.

In a finitely repeated game there is an incentive for each player to forego the mutually beneficial outcome of the nonequilibrium strategy of mutual cooperation. Generally, backward induction ensures that only actions yielding Nash equilibria in the single stage game are eligible to be included in the strategy path when the game is finite. The Cartesian product of the sets of actions yielding equilibria in each stage game denotes the number of possible paths to the equilibrium in the repeated game. Using backward induction, an equilbrium strategy for Z^3 must be subgame perfect. In the Prisoners' Dilemma game, the uniqueness of the Nash equilibria in each stage game leads to a unique subgame perfect equilibria in the finite game. Player 1 will choose the strategy $(\text{defect}^1, \text{defect}^2, \text{defect}^3)$ and Player 2's strategy will also be $(\text{defect}^1, \text{defect}^2, \text{defect}^3)$, such that the notation is that of $((s^1, s^2, s^3); (t^1, t^2, t^3))$, where s denotes the actions of Player 1 and t

denotes the actions of Player 2. Please note that the superscripts refer to a particular stage game and not to a player.

The only Nash equilibrium will be (defect[1], defect[2], defect[3]), since any strategy that calls for cooperation at any time can be ruled out.[33] However, what if the stage game does not have a dominant strategy equilibrium? The game of Chicken presented in Chapter 2 (presented again in Matrix 3.2) is one such game. In a three-iteration game, backward induction does not identify a single subgame perfect equilibrium, but it does help identify which strategy profiles will be subgame perfect. Where there are three Nash equilibria in the stage game (as derived in Chapter 2), the set of strategy profiles that will yield subgame perfection is the Cartesian product of the actions that yield Nash equilibria in each subgame. For a repeated game of Chicken[3], that gives us 27 subgame perfect strategy profiles based on the action sets of (contribute$_1$, not contribute$_2$), (not contribute$_1$, contribute$_2$), and (($\frac{1}{3}$contribute$_1$, $\frac{2}{3}$not contribute$_1$), ($\frac{1}{3}$contribute$_2$, $\frac{2}{3}$not contribute$_2$)) that are Nash equilibria in the stage game. For example, one such Nash equilibrium is (((not contribute$_1$, not contribute$_2$, ($\frac{1}{3}$contribute$_3$, $\frac{2}{3}$not contribute$_3$)); (contribute$_1$, contribute$_2$, ($\frac{1}{3}$contribute$_3$, $\frac{2}{3}$not contribute$_3$)))).

The strategies that can yield these 27 strategy profiles are more numerous since strategies in a repeated game are a function of both the actions in a stage game and the use of the history of the prior stage games. The use of prior history allows a player to make her actions in any stage game contingent on what the other player has done previously. For example, Player 1 may use a strategy that states that if Player 2 chooses not contribute in the stage game immediately prior, he, Player 1, will contribute in the current stage game, otherwise not contribute. Alternatively, Player 1 may say that once Player 2 has not contributed for two stage games in a row, she will choose contribute in the current stage game, otherwise not contribute. Both of these strategies could yield the same action in the third stage game

MATRIX 3.2

A Game of Chicken

| | | Player 2 | |
		Contribute	Not Contribute
Player 1	Contribute	2, 2	1, 4
	Not Contribute	4, 1	0, 0

if Player 2 had chosen not contribute in Chicken^1 and Chicken^2; they would yield different actions if Player 1 chose the action of contribute in Chicken^1 and not contribute in Chicken^2.

In the finite game, even though the equilibrium set of strategies (combining history with the possible actions) is very large, it is still limited to the 27 strategy profiles formed by the Cartesian product of the stage games' Nash equilibria.[34] Let us look at a couple of pure strategies that are subgame perfect for the iterated game of Chicken^3. The first equilibrium could be the result of the strategy profile ((not contribute^1, not contribute^2, not contribute^3); (contribute^1, contribute^2, contribute^3)), again where the notation is that of ((s^1, s^2, s^3); (t^1, t^2, t^3)), where s denotes the actions of Player 1 and t denotes the actions of Player 2. Of course, several strategies could yield these actions. This first equilibrium results from Player 1, GM, always choosing to not contribute and Player 2, Ford, always choosing to contribute. Neither player can unilaterally make itself better off in any stage game. Player 1 would receive a payoff of $4 + 4 + 4 = 12$ and Player 2 would receive a payoff of $1 + 1 + 1 = 3$.

There are other strategy profiles and thus strategies that are in equilibrium too. Player 1 and Player 2 could alternately contribute first. GM might say to Ford, "If you contribute first this year, I will do likewise tomorrow, although I will definitely not contribute on the third and last year." Ford could agree and play (contribute$_1$, not contribute$_2$, contribute$_3$) to GM's (not contribute$_1$, contribute$_2$, not contribute$_3$). So long as at each stage game neither player can unilaterally better themselves, there is an equilibrium. With finite repetition, the strategy profiles are limited to the set of subgame perfect strategies.

Infinitely Repeated Games

It may be the case, however, that people don't know when their mutual interaction is going to end. We may be involved in an interaction that is ongoing until further notice. There may be no clear horizon of when your interaction will come to an end. Your neighbor, husband, or colleague may be there for life for all you know. If that is the case, then we can think of the possibility of an infinitely repeated game. In this case, there is no final stage game from which to use backward induction. Typically, those people who are interested in the development of cooperative relationships are looking to model infinite interactions. We often ask the question in many fields of study: "Is it possible to develop cooperative or reciprocal relationships over the long term that are not possible in any single or finite interaction?" A person studying families may note altruism and cooperation among members in the provision of collective goods. Why is that? A person studying politics may find nations cooperating with each other over the long term in a way that does not seem predictive from any single-shot case.

Once you have an idea of an ongoing relationship without any clear ending, you lose the focusing effect of backward inductions. The need to choose in each subgame as if it is your last move disappears. As a result, an exponentially large increase in the number of potential equilibria occurs. This is largely because of the concept of updating information about another player's strategy that is possible through repeated interaction. One player's actions can communicate a strategy to a fellow player that is contingent on the fellow player's actions. This can lead to equilibrium strategy profiles that are not equilibria in the finite game.

Discounting

If the payoffs were truly just one infinite sum versus another, then one would be indifferent between any two choices of infinite sums since any number added an infinite number of times sums to infinity. Clearly, this does not seem to conform to expected behavior. To distinguish between the infinite sums, we utilize the concept of discounting. This well known concept says that people place different valuations on the future. Some people value tomorrow more than others. Some people may even value tomorrow equally with today, whereas others may take the *carpe diem* approach to life to an extreme.[35]

Suppose you knew you were going to sell your house in two years whereas your neighbor plans to stay for the foreseeable future. Both of you have maintained bluegrass lawns until this point. Each of you previously took turns stopping, digging, or killing any invading fescue grass along your property line. You were playing a game of repeated Chicken where you alternated playing the contribute, or dig it out, strategy. Knowing you are going to be moving out of the neighborhood, it probably doesn't concern you as much whether your mutual lawns will turn entirely into sharp-on-the-feet fescue in a few years.

Your neighbor, suspecting that you are going to be moving, starts to take unilateral action to control fescue along the fence line. You are happy because your house will show better on the market in two years, but your neighbor is more happy at stopping the invading sharp and unsightly grass long term. If she waits she will either have to replace her entire yard or learn to love fescue.

The parable of fescue introduces the idea of a discount rate. A neighbor who is planning to move may give less value to projects with a long-term payoff. Because of the differences in discount factors, one neighbor may be more likely than the other to bear the major share of costs. This would be true of any repeated Chicken game that was used to model the provision of a public good by one player. To leave suburbia and reenter the world of 1950s teen angst, it may be the case that Jimmy's discount factor in a repeated game is much greater than Buzz's. We already know that Jimmy had been moved from town to town by his anxious parents. Although he may like to be considered as cool as Buzz in Susie's eyes, he knows that she is just one more girl along the way. Buzz, knowing that Jimmy has a high discount rate, believes that Jimmy may be more susceptible to his announcement that he intends to not jump. Differential valuations of time can alter how the payoffs from future interactions are valued.

Your payoffs, then, depend on the infinite stream of payoffs from the stage games in the game. Player 1's payoff stream would depend on his evaluation of the resulting strategy profile over the infinite stage games, $n = 1, 2, \ldots$:

$$u_i(s_1, t_1) + r_i u_i(s_2, t_2) + r_i^2 u_i(s_3, t_3) + \cdots + r_i^{n-1} u_i(s_n, t_n) + \cdots$$

where r_i is the discount rate, $0 < r_i < 1$, that Player i applies to future payoffs.

A discount rate models how highly a person values the future as compared to the present. A person with a discount rate close to 0 only cares about today. A person with a discount rate equal to 1 would be just as happy to receive one million dollars in the future as she would be to receive it today. An infinite series of equal amounts allows us to use a mathematical identity to simplify the discount rate where

$$1 + r + r^2 + r^3 + \cdots = 1/(1 - r)$$

If GM played not contribute always and Ford played always contribute, GM's payoff for the game would look like

$$u_{GM}(\text{not contribute always}_{GM}|\text{always contribute}_F)$$

$$= 4 + r_{GM}(4) + r_{GM}^2(4) + \cdots \quad \text{or} \quad \frac{4}{(1 - r_{GM})}$$

whereas Ford would receive the payoff

$$u_F(\text{always contribute}_F|\text{not contribute always}_{GM})$$

$$= 1 + r_F 1 + r_F^2 1 \cdots \quad \text{or} \quad \frac{1}{(1 - r_F)}$$

If the discount rate approaches 1, then the payoff of the repeated game approaches the summation of the payoffs from the stage games. As the discount rate approaches 0, the value of payoffs in the future becomes less valuable to the point where any payoff beyond today doesn't matter. Since we are interested in the development of reciprocal relationships, we usually investigate situations where the discount rate is high. Otherwise, we would be looking at relationships where a person with every encounter treats the other person as new and without any history.

The most written about and perhaps most intuitively satisfying repeated infinite game is that of the Prisoners' Dilemma. Axelrod (1984) and Taylor (1987) closely explored the creation of strategy profiles in the repeated game which lead to mutual cooperation. The strategy combination of two players both playing always cooperate will never be an equilibrium in the infinite game because each faces an incentive to defect to receive a higher payoff. However, there are other more subtle ways to achieve cooperation where we can use contingent strategies to reward cooperation and punish defections. Strategies such as always cooperate until the other player defects and then always defect forevermore, often referred to as a grim trigger strategy, can lead to an incentive to cooperate under certain conditions. If someone is playing this strategy, then it is a weak best response to play the same strategy. The short-term advantage of defecting against such a strategy is outweighed by the long-term loss of the mutual cooperation payoff for all but the lowest of discount rates.

In an infinitely repeated game of Chicken, it may be the case that a strategy where both players choose contribute can work as well. Without knowing when the interaction will end, it may be the case that it could be valuable for both players to contribute for a period of time. GM and Ford may decide that if they each contribute every year, then neither gets ahead. We could imagine a contingent strategy of a grim trigger strategy that states as long as Player 2 contributes, I will contribute; once Player 2 plays not contribute, I will not contribute forever. For simplicity, we will refer to this strategy as Grim Chicken. This strategy would be similar to the grim strategy mentioned previously in connection with the Prisoners' Dilemma game. Here, we might want to try to induce the acceptance of the mediocre outcome $(2, 2)$ every year rather than the competitive outcome of $(4, 1)$ or $(1, 4)$ or the deficient outcome of $(0, 0)$. By both playing Grim Chicken (GC), each player will get the following stream of payoffs:

$$u_2(GC_2|GC_1) = 2 + r(2) + r^2(2) + \cdots + r^n(2) + \cdots \quad \text{or} \quad 2\left(\frac{1}{1-r}\right).$$

If a player were to deviate from this cooperative effort against the Grim Chicken strategy at the $n+1$ stage game, then the deviant would immediately get the initial superior pay off of not contributing while the other contributed, but then receive the deficient payoff of mutual not contributing thereafter.

$$u_2(\text{deviant}_2|GC_1): 2 + r(2) + r^2(2) + \cdots + r^n(4) + r^{n+1}(0) + r^{n+2}(0) + \cdots$$

In order to know if it is beneficial for a person to not contribute once a game of Grim Chicken has started, we can compare the differences between the two payoff streams and solve for r. This approach would be appropriate for comparing any two payoff streams. If $u_2(GC_2|GC_1) > u_2(\text{deviant}_2|GC_1)$, no one would rationally choose to play deviant:

$$u_2(GC_2|GC_1) - u_2(\text{deviant}_2|GC_1)$$
$$= (2-4)r^n + (2-0)r^{n+1} + (2-0)r^{n+2} + (2-0)r^{n+3} + \cdots$$

$$0 = r^{n+1}[(2-4)r^{-1} + (2-0) + (2-0)r + (2-0)r^2 + \cdots]$$

$$0 = r^{n+1}\left[-2r^{-1} + 2\left(\frac{1}{1-r}\right)\right]$$

$$0 = \frac{-2}{r} + \frac{2}{(1-r)}$$

$$0 = -2(1-r) + 2r$$

$$2 = 6r$$

$$\tfrac{1}{3} = r$$

So long as the discount rate is $\frac{1}{3}$ or higher, the deviant strategy would not payoff for the player and she would be better off continuing in the mutual strategy of contingent contributing.

Now of course, two neighbors trading turns week by week on the fence line could be better off. This scenario is the equivalent of playing Tit-for-Tat to Tat-for-Tit in the many descriptions of the repeated Prisoners' Dilemma game. Tit-for-Tat (TFT) is a contingent strategy where one player will cooperate (here contribute) on the first move and then play what the other player just played in the $n-1$ stage game on all succeeding moves. Tat-for-Tit (TFT') is the reverse, where one player defects (here does not contribute) on the first move and plays what the action of the other player was in the most recent stage game ($n-1$). In a game of Chicken, this leads to an alteration of responsibilities and benefits. Look at the stream of payoffs for the Tit-for-Tat player to examine how this works

$$u_1(\text{TFT}_1|\text{TFT}_2') = 1 + r(4) + r^2(1) + r^3(4) + r^4(1)\cdots$$

The player starting with Tat-for-Tit would get the immediate payoff of 4 and then alternate thereafter, yielding the payoff stream

$$u_2(\text{TFT}_2'|\text{TFT}_1) = 4 + r(1) + r^2(4) + r^3(1) + r^4(4)\cdots$$

We know that this strategy is an equilibrium because it is a subgame perfect strategy even in the finite game. To see if there is any incentive to deviate from it in the infinite setting, imagine what happens if the Tat-for-Tit player tries to always not contribute at any even-numbered,

$n + 1$ stage game. The deviation would produce the following payoff stream for the deviant:

$$u_2(D_2|\text{TFT}_1) = 4 + r(1) + r^2(4) + \cdots + r^{n-1}(4)$$
$$+ r^n(4) + r^{n+1}(0) + r^{n+2}(0) \cdots$$

The difference between the two strategies is

$$u_2(D_2|\text{TFT}_1) - u_2(\text{TFT}_2'|\text{TFT}_1) = r^n\{3 - 4(r) - 1(r^2) - 4(r^3) - 1(r^4) \cdots\}$$

How would we know whether it is worthwhile to stay with TFT' or move to the deviant strategy? Can we imagine a case in the infinite game where moving off a subgame perfect strategy in the finite case is worthwhile? Well, it depends on the person's discount rate and whether that extra immediate payoff of 4 in the $n + 1$ game is worth the following series of zeroes. Imagine that for a low enough discount rate this might be true. As we can see, solving for these problems gets complicated in a hurry. What is important is that by varying the discount rates, the number of equilibrium strategies increases.

Adding infinity to our time horizon allows for an incredible explosion in the number of equilibria. We will explore the consequences of these additional equilibria after we first examine a finite game with a given probability of ending.

Finite Games With a Given Probability of Ending

Infinite games are often criticized as being unrealistic. So long as a person is interacting with another person in the good faith expectation that they will be seeing them again, the concept of never-ending or infinity seems appropriate. However, what if each interaction is filled with some wariness regarding whether the person will be seeing the other again? Suppose, either Ford or GM suddenly went bankrupt. It has happened before to other auto giants (e.g., AMC), so why not again? Your neighbor today may not be your neighbor tomorrow. How does this expectation that a relationship may come to an end affect equilibria?

This situation is typically modelled as a finite game where the probability of any stage game being the last game is greater than 0 but less than 1. Consider the case of the yearly Chicken game where GM may go out of business on any given day. Let's say that each year that GM and Ford meet there is only a 75% probability that they will meet again. At the beginning of the game, the probability that Ford and GM will meet for the nth game is $\left(\frac{3}{4}\right)^{n-1}$. Suppose that each had chosen the strategy of Grim Chicken. This cooperative strategy would now yield an expected payoff stream modified by the expected probability of meeting again. Each player's expected payoff (minus any discount consideration) will be

$$u_{GM}(GC_{GM}|GC_F) = 2 + \left(\tfrac{3}{4}\right)2 + \left(\tfrac{3}{4}\right)^2 2 + \cdots + \left(\tfrac{3}{4}\right)^{n-1}2$$
$$+ \left(\tfrac{3}{4}\right)^n 2 + \left(\tfrac{3}{4}\right)^{n+1}2 + \cdots$$

If GM gets tired of contributing every year and turns to the deviant strategy of always not contributing at the $n+1$ stage game, can GM benefit? If it does deviate it gets

$$u_{GM}(D_{GM}|GC_F) = 2 + \left(\tfrac{3}{4}\right)2 + \left(\tfrac{3}{4}\right)^2 2 + \cdots + \left(\tfrac{3}{4}\right)^{n-1}2$$
$$+ \left(\tfrac{3}{4}\right)^n 4 + \left(\tfrac{3}{4}\right)^{n+1}0 + \cdots$$

GM will not deviate if $u_{GM}(GC_{GM}|GC_F) \geq u_{GM}(D_{GM}|GC_F)$. GM will compare the two strategies to see if $u_{GM}(GC_{GM}|GC_F) - u_{GM}(D_{GM}|GC_F)$ is positive. It gets the comparison

$$u_{GM}(GC_{GM}|GC_F) - u_{GM}(D_{GM}|GC_F)$$
$$= (2-4)\left(\tfrac{3}{4}\right)^n + (2-0)\left(\tfrac{3}{4}\right)^{n+1} + (2-0)\left(\tfrac{3}{4}\right)^{n+2} + \cdots$$
$$= \left(\tfrac{3}{4}\right)^n \left[-2 + 2\left(\tfrac{3}{4}\right) + 2\left(\tfrac{3}{4}\right)^2 + \cdots\right]$$
$$= \left(\tfrac{3}{4}\right)^n \left[-2 + 2\left(\frac{\tfrac{3}{4}}{(1-\tfrac{3}{4})}\right)\right]$$
$$= \left(\tfrac{3}{4}\right)^n (-2 + 6) = \left(\tfrac{3}{4}\right)^n 4 \geq 0$$

Even if GM thinks that Ford will go bankrupt with a 25% probability, Ford still would be better off staying with its cooperative mutual contribute strategy given Ford's choice to play Grim Chicken.

Finite games with a known probability of ending work similarly to infinite games with discounting. The probability of ending is a close relative to the discount rate. Both affect how you would value future interactions.

The Folk Theorem

The change from a finite game to either an infinite game or a finite game with a known probability of ending creates a plethora of equilibrium strategies. Infinity begets infinity. Infinite stage games lead to infinite strategies. In fact, game theorists have shown that under certain conditions there can be a very large number of equilibria.

The Folk theorem tells us that in infinite games that allow for discounting, the number of strategies that can qualify as an equilibrium is very large.[36] One good characterization of the Folk theorem was given by Ordeshook (1992, pp. 179–180):

> In an infinitely repeated game, any outcome that gives each player what that player can guarantee for himself if he plays the game without coordinating with anyone else—any outcome that satisfies the security value of each player—can correspond to an equilibrium.

In order to understand this, we must look at what a security value is. In the single-shot game of Chicken, Player 2 will at the least get a payoff of 1 if he contributes and 0 if he doesn't contribute. His security value is 1, which is the most he can guarantee himself by his own choice alone. In a repeated game, Player 2's security level is the discounted sum of the payoff of 1 in each subgame. The Folk theorem says that there are a variety of ways in an infinite setting to guarantee one's security level. Because of an infinite horizon, any cooperation could withstand a defection so long as the possibility exists that the resulting punishment could lower the defector's average payoff in some finite series of stage games to be below the defectors security level.[37] Also, there would need to be a redemption period where renewed cooperation can make up for the costs of punishment. For example, in the Chicken game where two players were cooperating in cleaning up the fence line and one chose to defect to let the other do it, there probably will exist some sequence of punishments, in this case with a payoff of (0, 0), that will more than detract from the advantage of the momentary defections. Redemption occurs when a stream of resulting advantageous cooperation beyond the punishment cycle more than makes up for the cost incurred by the player who does the punishing. If the sequence of cooperation fall from grace, punishment, and redemption were infinitely followed, a strategy would be in equilibria.[38]

The key is an appropriate punishment period that negates the advantage of defection and is followed by a period of redemption that reimburses the punisher for her costs. If we look at infinite games as a series of these finite sequences, we can imagine there are many different ways to fall from grace, to be punished, to be saved, and to be redeemed. Depending on the structure of the stage game and the relative valuation differences between the payoffs, there will be more or fewer ways to enter heaven. Where infinity is a long time, the length of these sequences can vary and that variation alone pushes up the number of potential equilibria. The only other variable is the discount rate. If it is too low, the sequence of Eden, the fall, the punishment, and the redemption may be too long to be fully valued.

In an infinitely repeated game, we not only have the equilibria that were subgame perfect in the finite game, we also have the wide variety of these contingent punishment sequences that can result from equilibria. This creates either an opportunity or a problem to someone who would use game theory to model repeated interactions. The opportunity is that the Folk theorem tells us to look for this type of sequence as an alternative to more straightforward pure strategies. In the case of the Prisoners' Dilemma or Chicken, the opportunity tells us that there may be many ways by which cooperation can be assured. The problem, for some, is that there is no clear and easy one way to characterize cooperation.

Conclusion

In this chapter we explored the concept of repeated interaction between two players. We defined the concept of repeated games, introduced notation and terminology, and characterized equilibria in the finite and infinitely repeated settings. In the finite settings we saw that equilibria will be subgame perfect because of the logic of backward induction. No strategy can be played that plays an action that would not yield a Nash equilibria in the single stage game. In the infinite setting, equilibria that are not subgame perfect can result because of the loss of the threat of that last end-game. Some of these equilibria are sensitive to changes in the discount rate. The finitely repeated game, with a known probability of ending, can also support non-subgame perfect equilibria dependent on the probability of the game ending at any stage game. Finally, the Folk theorem tells us that the number of Nash equilibria in any infinite game can be quite large. Also, we can characterize the requirements of this potentially large group of equilibria as those where a player can guarantee himself his security value in a finite sequence of stage games. By looking at the potential sequences where a player can rationally punish (that is, achieve his/her discounted security level), we can start to investigate and appreciate the diverse ways by which cooperation or reciprocity can be contingently assured.

4. N-PLAYER GAMES

Three Is a Crowd

Consider again Buzz and Jimmy sitting across from each other in their respective stolen cars. Now suppose that just as they are about to agree to settle their differences with a "Chickie Run" game, along comes Plato in a very fine stolen coupe. Both Buzz and Jimmy have had separate altercations with Plato. After some exchange of words, they all eventually agree to play "Chickie Run" against one another as a means of settling their disputes. We now have a three-player game. The rules are essentially the same as the game between Buzz and Jimmy, but now there are three players. That is, all three teenagers race together toward the cliff, jumping too soon is awarded with being called "chicken," and waiting too long results in death. How does the addition of Plato (a third player) change the game?

How about our Chicken lobbying game played between Ford and GM? How does the game change when we consider the strategic actions of Chrysler? Again the rules of the game are essentially the same as before. The car companies have two choices: to contribute to a lobbying effort or to not contribute. In this chapter, we examine some three-player versions of this Chicken game introduced in Chapter 2. We then turn to an analysis of several N-player versions of this game. Later we examine N-player sequential games that involve repeated play between a large number of players.

Three-Player Chicken Games

In developing a three-player version of Chicken, several characteristics of the two-player game need to be preserved. These qualities include the two following:

1. All players prefer that everyone contributes rather than everyone does not contribute; that is, for Ford, $[u_F = (\text{contribute}_{GM}; \text{contribute}_F; \text{contribute}_C)] > [u_F = (\text{not contribute}_{GM}; \text{not contribute}_F; \text{not contribute}_C)]$.
2. Each player's most preferred outcome is to be the only one who did not contribute; that is, for Ford, $u_F^{\max} = (\text{contribute}_{GM}; \text{not contribute}_F; \text{contribute}_C)$.

These two criteria serve to define all Chicken games whether two player, three player, or N player. In addition, we have the following characteristics:

3. All players play the game with imperfect and complete information. As in previous chapters, we relax these assumptions later in this chapter.
4. For this variation of the three-player Chicken game, each player prefers to not contribute if the other two contribute and to contribute if any of the other two players does not contribute. That is, for Ford, $[u_F = (\text{contribute}_{GM}; \text{ not contribute}_F; \text{ contribute}_C)] > [u_F = (\text{contribute}_{GM}; \text{ contribute}_F; \text{ contribute}_C)]$ and $[u_F = (\text{contribute}_{GM}; \text{ contribute}_F; \text{ not contribute}_C)] > [u_F = (\text{contribute}_{GM}; \text{ not contribute}_F; \text{ not contribute}_C)]$.

We will slightly modify this fourth characteristic later in this chapter.

Matrix 4.1 shows a version of the Chicken game that is defined by these four characteristics. Matrix 4.1 represents a simple three-by-three game with complete and imperfect information. As with the game presented in Chapter 2, each player has two strategies: contribute or not contribute. Rather than try to prepare a three dimensional matrix, we present a two-by-four matrix, whereby the two-by-two matrix of the game played between Ford and GM is doubled by Chrysler's choice of contribute or not contribute. Each cell contains three payoffs. The leftmost payoff is assigned to GM, then comes Ford's payoff, and all the way to the right is Chrysler's payoff. Thus the upper left-hand cell has an outcome of (contribute$_{GM}$; contribute$_F$; contribute$_C$) and payoffs of $(2, 2, 2)$. The lower left-hand cell has an outcome of (not contribute$_{GM}$; not contribute$_F$; not contribute$_C$) and payoffs of $(0, 0, 0)$. The upper right-hand cell has an outcome of (contribute$_{GM}$; not contribute$_F$; not contribute$_C$) and payoffs of $(-1, 0, 0)$. The preference ordering exhibits the qualities of the Chicken game for the three players.

MATRIX 4.1
A Game of Three-Player Chicken with Imperfect
Information—Variation 1

| Chrysler | | Contribute | | Not Contribute | |
Ford		Contribute	Not Contribute	Contribute	Not Contribute
GM	Contribute	2, 2, 2	1, 4, 1	1, 1, 4	−1, 0, 0
	Not Contribute	4, 1, 1	0, 0, −1	0, −1, 0	0, 0, 0

There exist four Nash equilibria for the three-player Chicken game:

$$(\text{contribute}_{GM};\ \text{not contribute}_{F};\ \text{contribute}_{C})$$

$$(\text{not contribute}_{GM};\ \text{contribute}_{F};\ \text{contribute}_{C})$$

$$(\text{contribute}_{GM};\ \text{contribute}_{F};\ \text{not contribute}_{C})$$

and

$$\left(\left(\tfrac{1}{3}\text{contribute}_{GM},\ \tfrac{2}{3}\text{not contribute}_{GM}\right);\right.$$

$$\left(\tfrac{1}{3}\text{contribute}_{F},\ \tfrac{2}{3}\text{not contribute}_{F}\right)$$

$$\left.\left(\tfrac{1}{3}\text{contribute}_{C},\ \tfrac{2}{3}\text{not contribute}_{C}\right)\right).[39]$$

Compare this mixed strategy Nash equilibrium to that of the two-player Chicken game. In the two-player game, the mixed strategy Nash equilibrium is

$$\left(\left(\tfrac{1}{3}\text{contribute}_{GM},\ \tfrac{2}{3}\text{not contribute}_{GM}\right);\right.$$

$$\left.\left(\tfrac{1}{3}\text{contribute}_{F},\ \tfrac{2}{3}\text{not contribute}_{F}\right)\right).$$

In terms of each players' mix of strategies, there is little difference between the three-player game and the two-player game. Clearly the -1 payoff makes a difference. There really is no equivalent payoff associated with the two-player game. In the two-player game, contributing yet not producing the public good leads to a payoff of 0. In this three-player game, contributing while the other two free-ride produces a less desirable outcome. Nonetheless, we see from this example that adding a player to the game need not make a big difference in terms of equilibrium strategies.

The particular mix of strategies in this Nash equilibrium results from the preference orderings that each of the players assigns to the different outcomes of this game. In particular they result from characteristic 4 of three-player Chicken games listed above. What happens if we modify this characteristic? That is, we now consider a three-player game where each player prefers to not contribute if at least one player has chosen to contribute, and to contribute only if both of the other two players do not contribute. We call this version 2 of three-player Chickie Run. We modify each firm's preferences. For example, we modify Ford's preferences as follows:

$$[u_F = (\text{contribute}_{GM};\ \text{not contribute}_F;\ \text{not contribute}_C)]$$
$$> [u_F = (\text{contribute}_{GM};\ \text{contribute}_F;\ \text{contribute}_C)]$$

and

$$[u_F = (\text{not contribute}_{GM};\ \text{contribute}_F;\ \text{not contribute}_C)]$$
$$> [u_F = (\text{not contribute}_{GM};\ \text{not contribute}_F;\ \text{not contribute}_C)]$$

Essentially this means that in version 2 of this three-player game, instead of one player deterring contributing, only two players can deter contributing.

Matrix 4.2 presents the normal form game of this modified version of three-player Chicken. The major difference in payoffs to the players playing this game is evident when two players choose not contribute while one player selects contribute; the corresponding payoffs are (1, 4, 4), (4, 1, 4), and (4, 4, 1). As with the version 1 of the game, if all three players choose to not contribute, the payoff to each respective player is (0, 0, 0); likewise, if all players contribute, the payoff is (2, 2, 2). The four Nash equilibria for version 2 of the three-player Chicken game are

(contribute$_{GM}$; not contribute$_F$; not contribute$_C$)

(not contribute$_{GM}$; contribute$_F$; not contribute$_C$)

(not contribute$_{GM}$; not contribute$_F$; contribute$_C$)

MATRIX 4.2
A Game of Three-Player Chicken with Imperfect
Information—Variation 2

		Contribute		Not Contribute	
Chrysler Ford		Contribute	Not Contribute	Contribute	Not Contribute
GM	Contribute	2, 2, 2	1, 4, 1	1, 1, 4	1, 4, 4
	Not Contribute	4, 1, 1	4, 4, 1	4, 1, 4	0, 0, 0

and

$$((0.1367 \text{ contribute}_{GM}, 0.8633 \text{ not contribute}_{GM});$$
$$(0.1367 \text{ contribute}_{F}, 0.8633 \text{ not contribute}_{F});$$
$$(0.1367 \text{ contribute}_{C}, 0.8633 \text{ not contribute}_{C}))[40]$$

This means that a player's mixed strategy equilibrium strategy will be to contribute around 14% of the time.

This second variation of Chicken in many respects better serves as a model of the collective action problem seen in the lobbying efforts of Ford, GM, and Chrysler than as a model of Buzz, Jimmy, and Plato racing their cars toward the cliff in a three-player "Chickie Run" game. The reason for this is that by altering the preference ordering, we have reduced the danger of two players racing toward the brink of the cliff after the third player has jumped. In this way this version of the game fails to account for the brinkmanship evident in the game between two players. As a model of collective action, this variation of three-player Chicken fares better.

Version 2 of Chicken produces a higher probability of each player not contributing than we saw in version 1 of Chicken (Matrix 4.1). If we think of version 1 of Chicken as a collective action problem, it is evident that two of the three players are required to maintain a successful lobbying effort. More specifically, version 1 of the three-player Chicken game induces a mixed equilibrium strategy of contributing about 58% of the time, while version 2 leads to contributing at a rate of around 14%. In this respect we see that by modifying characteristic 4 of three-player chicken, we alter the mixed strategy Nash equilibrium. Furthermore, this modification of the game demonstrates that the addition of players alone may alter the equilibrium mixed strategies.

N-Player Chicken Games

Many social, economic, and political strategic actions involve more than two or three players. We have already seen how adding an additional player to the Chickie Run game altered the equilibria. In this section we examine the effect of adding an indeterminant ("N" additional players) to a game.[41]

At this point maintaining our story of "Chickie Run" with an indeterminant number of N players becomes problematic. We could develop a weird tale of a score of teenagers all gathered near a cliff prepared to use each of their respective stolen cars to play N-player Chickie Run, but such a game seems too fantastic and bizarre. Such a game might be a bit too similar to tales of lemmings throwing themselves over a cliff. Instead, we slightly alter our monopolistically competitive three firm collective action Chicken game to an N-player game. With this game we can preserve the characteristics described in the two variations of the three-player Chicken game. We consider here a lumpy public good, one which requires that some number k contribute to the lobbying effort.[42] If fewer than k players contribute, the lobbying effort will be unsuccessful.

For the N-player game we consider the following generalized qualities:

1. All players prefer that the lobbying effort be successful; that is, that all players prefer that at least k players choose to contribute rather than having $k - 1$ or fewer players choose to contribute.
2. Each player prefers to not contribute rather than contribute as long as k players are contributing to the lobbying effort.
3. All players play this game with complete and imperfect information. Players thus must assign some subjective probability, P, to any other player's propensity for contributing as opposed to not contributing.

Matrix 4.3 shows the outcomes and payoffs associated with player i's choices with respect to what k other players choose.[43] Each row in this matrix shows the outcome and payoff for i associated with different levels of contribute and not contribute chosen by the other players. The first column shows the outcomes and payoffs to i associated with $k - 2$ or fewer other players choosing to contribute to the lobbying effort. Whether i chooses to contribute or to not contribute, the lobbying effort will not be successful, regardless. In terms of i's payoffs this means there will be no benefit from lobbying and if i chooses to contribute, the only payoff will be the cost of contributing to lobbying (fruitlessly).

The second column in Matrix 4.3 shows the outcome and payoffs associated with precisely $k - 1$ players choosing to contribute. This means that player i is critical to the production of the lumpy public good. If i chooses to contribute, lobbying is successful. If i chooses

MATRIX 4.3
N-Player Game of Chicken

		$k-2$ Others Contribute	$k-1$ Others Contribute	k Others Contribute
Player 1	Contribute	Public Good Not Produced $-c$	Public Good Produced $b-c$	Public Good Produced $b-c$
	Not Contribute	Public Good Not Produced 0	Public Good Not Produced 0	Public Good Produced b

to shirk (not contribute), lobbying will be unsuccessful. Contributing provides i with a payoff of b, the benefit derived from successful lobbying minus the cost of contribution c, $(b - c)$. Not contributing provides nothing since there is no cost, but then again there is no change in policy either. The third column shows what happens when k or more other players choose to contribute. If i chooses to contribute, i receives the benefit from the public good minus the cost of contributing, $(b - c)$. If i chooses to not contribute, i can enjoy the benefits of successful lobbying while free-riding on the efforts of others, thereby receiving a payoff of b. Clearly for player i, the most preferred outcome is to shirk (not contribute) while k other players choose to contribute. The least preferred outcome is to contribute while $k - 2$ other players choose to not contribute. Such a game exhibits all the characteristics of a Chicken game discussed previously.

What is the equilibrium strategy in such an N-player Chicken game? This can be calculated by taking the expected payoffs associated with i's decision to contribute or shirk. Critical to this calculation are the different subjective probabilities regarding the number of players deciding to contribute to lobbying. The expected payoff for working then is

$$u_i(\text{contribute}) = P_{k-2}(-c) + P_{k-1}(b - c) + P_k(b - c)$$

where P_{k-2} is the probability that fewer than two other players (not including i) are needed to successfully lobby choose to contribute, P_{k-1} is the probability that i is the critical provider of the lobbying effort, and P_k means that k players other than i choose to contribute. Of course, the sum of these three probabilities is 1. The expected payoff of shirking is

$$u_i(\text{not contribute}) = P_k(b)$$

since all other payoffs associated with not contributing are 0. When the $u_i(\text{work}) > u_i(\text{shirk})$, i works to produce the good. When $u_i(\text{contribute}) < u_i(\text{not contribute})$, i chooses to not contribute. To find the mixed strategy Nash equilibrium, we set $u_i(\text{contribute}) = u_i(\text{not contribute})$.[44] This simplifies to

$$P_{k-1}(b) - (c)$$

In turn, the probability that i is the critical (kth) contributor equals the ratio between the benefits derived from lobbying and the costs of lobbying,

$$P_{k-1} = c/b$$

The probability of i being the critical contributor then is directly related to the ratio of costs and benefits associated with lobbying for a change in policy.

To calculate the actual mixed strategy Nash equilibrium for this game we must take into account the number of groups of k within the population of N that are needed to produce the lumpy public good (the lobbying effort). This can be expressed in the binomial term $\binom{N-1}{k-1}$.[45] By setting the difference $u_i(\text{contribute}) - u_i(\text{not contribute}) = D$, we can calculate the expected payoff differential between contributing and not contributing, such that

$$D = (b)\binom{N-1}{k-1}P^{k-1}(1-P)^{N-k} - (c)$$

Player i will contribute if $D > 0$ and not contribute if $D < 0$. From this equation it is evident that the mixed strategy Nash equilibrium for this N-player Chicken game is affected by the relative size of k compared to N, the probability of i being the critical contributor (P_{k-1}), and the ratio of costs and benefits.[46]

It is quite evident that adding more players to a game does affect the game. So far in our three-player and N-player games we have only analyzed games played "simultaneously" or with complete and imperfect information. We now turn to a different variety of N-player game where each player plays a two-player game in a series of iterations or stages. We first present a sequential game in which a set of players plays a repeated game against the same opponent. Then we consider round-robin tournaments in which all players play against each other in iterated two-player Chicken games.

Sequential Games With N Players

Sequential games with N players are quite similar to repeated games. In fact, much of the early game-theoretic literature on reputation involved repeated games involving several actors playing against a single player who worked at establishing a reputation.[47] For our purposes we will continue to use the game of Chicken as our base model to explore this topic.

Information plays a big role in defining such games. As a means of explicating this point, we will focus our discussion in this section on three-player games with occasional references to N-player generalizations. Let us begin by assuming that all players in a three-player Chicken game possess complete and imperfect information. Such a game is portrayed in extensive form in Figure 4.1. Here information sets link all the decision nodes for Ford and Chrysler. None of the players knows what the others will do (or have done); the game is essentially played simultaneously and is equivalent to the game presented in Matrix 4.1.

Now consider Figure 4.2. In this three-player game, GM and Ford play their two-player game and then at some later time, GM plays Chrysler. An information set connects Ford's decision nodes; Ford plays an imperfect and complete information game with GM. Chrysler also plays an imperfect and complete information game with GM, but does know the outcome of GM's game with Ford. For such a game, each round of the game is a subgame since imperfect information connects the players' decision nodes. The payoffs associated with the first subgame played between GM and Ford are represented in the first line of payoffs. GM's payoff is listed first; then comes Ford's. The second line of payoffs matches the second subgame played between GM and Chrysler. Again GM's payoff comes first, followed by Chrysler's. The equilibria for this game is different than the three-player imperfect information game (that is, the game represented in Matrix 4.1 and Figure 4.1).

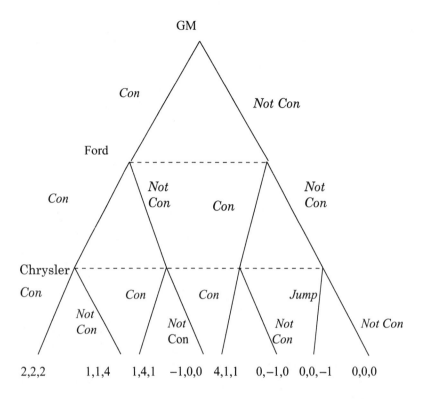

Figure 4.1. Three-Player Chicken With Imperfect Information—Variation 1

The perfect equilibria for the game presented in Figure 4.2 are similar to a two-player Chicken game for each round of the game. That is, for a three-player game, the last round of the game has Nash equilibria of (contribute$_{GM}$; not contribute$_C$), (not contribute$_{GM}$; contribute$_C$), and $\left(\left(\frac{1}{3}\text{contribute}_{GM}, \frac{2}{3}\text{not contribute}_{GM}\right); \left(\frac{1}{3}\text{contribute}_C, \frac{2}{3}\text{not contribute}_C\right)\right)$. A similar set of equilibria is evident in the first round. If the game were extended to finite N players, these Nash equilibria would hold for all rounds (subgames of the game). In other words, the equilibrium that holds in each subgame holds throughout the supergame.

What happens if Chrysler and Ford are uncertain about GM's type? In other words, what happens in a three-player game of Chicken with incomplete information? Here reputation can play a role in how

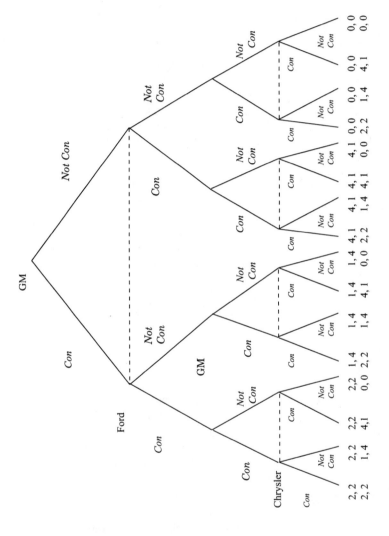

Figure 4.2. Three-Player Stage Game of Chicken With Imperfect Information

Chrysler plays the game against GM. This is the essential point be-hind Kreps and Wilson's (1982) examination of Selten's chain-store paradox. In our case, assume that GM can be either of two types: a hawk or a dove.[48] If GM is a dove, it will choose the strategy all con-tribute, meaning that it will contribute every time it plays the game. If GM is a hawk, its strategy will be all not contribute and it will play not contribute every time it plays the game. This game is represented in Figure 4.3. The problem for Chrysler is to determine whether or not GM is a hawk or a dove. Fortunately for Chrysler, it can observe what GM did in the previous round when it played Ford. This obser-vation allows Chrysler to update its beliefs about GM's propensity to be a hawk. Again as we saw in Chapter 2 we turn to Bayes' rule to

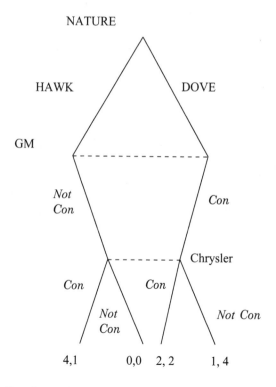

Figure 4.3. One Stage of Chicken Game With Incomplete and Imperfect In-formation

update beliefs as follows:

$$P(\text{hawk}|\text{no contribute})$$

$$= \frac{P(\text{no contribute}) \, P(\text{hawk})}{[P(\text{no contribute}|\text{hawk})P(\text{hawk}) + P(\text{no contribute}|\text{dove})P(\text{dove})]}$$

where P is Chrysler's belief and hawk is the propensity for GM to be a hawk. If Chrysler sees that GM plays no contribute against Ford, it will update its beliefs as follows:

$$P(\text{hawk}|\text{no contribute}) = \frac{(1) \, P(\text{hawk})}{(1)P(\text{hawk}) + (0)P(\text{dove})} = 1$$

By observing how GM played against Ford, Chrysler is able to update confidently. If GM plays no contribute against Ford, Chrysler knows GM's type is hawk. Since hawks play all no contribute, Chrysler then updates its belief confidently concluding that GM is a hawk.

Conclusion

What we learn from this consideration of N-player games is that there is considerable difference across different forms of N-player games. N-player games played virtually simultaneously (with imperfect information) provide valuable insights into group dynamics regarding collective actions problems and the provision of lumpy public goods. Tournaments—repeated two-player games played between a population of players—provide us insight into the nature of competing strategies in different environments.

NOTES

1. The reader should note that we have excluded material covered in Zagare's Chapters 2 and 4. Chapter 2 concerns zero-sum games. At present, these games are seldom used in the social sciences and, as such, the reader does not need to concern him/herself with this information. Chapter 4 concerns N-person cooperative games. For the most part, cooperative game theory is not used in the social sciences. Instead, the focus is on noncooperative game theory. Given this focus, we will only discuss topics from the more generalized noncooperative framework.

2. We are especially partial to Chapter 2 of Gates and Humes (1997).

3. We follow the standard of listing the row players payoff first and then the payoff of the column payoff.

4. This logic, which is called backward induction, will be examined more thoroughly in Chapter 3.

5. The discount rate refers to the value that a player places in receiving a payoff in the future versus the present. As we move farther into the future, we would expect a player to value equal payoffs less and less at later periods.

6. Cooperation may also result if the game is repeated a finite number of times with a probabilistic stopping point.

7. This result derives from the Folk theorem, which we discuss in greater detail in Chapter 3.

8. Besides the solution proposed in the text, others have suggested the following. The follower may have doubts about whether the leader has an option to acquiesce or to punish a rebellion. Other factors might rule out this choice for the leader.

9. In economics, the entire body of entry deterrence (chain-store paradox) games possess many similar properties to these leadership games. See, for example, Selten (1978), Kreps and Wilson (1982), Milgrom and Roberts (1982), and Fudenberg and Maskin (1986).

10. See Fearon (1994) for a related discussion concerning extended deterrence.

11. Of course, some people may say that the "Chickie Run" situation is not equivalent to the game of Chicken. We will address these concerns throughout the text.

12. See Schelling (1966) for his classic version of this game along with his additions to it.

13. Other scholars model MAD using games based on Chicken (Brams, 1985; Brams and Kilgour, 1988; Powell, 1987). Zagare (1985) argued that MAD should be modelled as a Prisoners' Dilemma game.

14. See Fink, Humes, and Schwebach (1997) concerning the connection between the size of alliance and alliance type.

15. See Cohen (1995).

16. The payoffs represented here are assigned cardinal values that reflect this ordinal ranking. Later in this chapter we will introduce more generalized payoffs for this game.

17. These strategies available to Ford and GM correspond to the choices jump and not jump presented to Jimmy and Buzz in the movie version of the Chickie Run game or for the strategies swerve and not swerve of the more common versions of the Chicken game.

18. Player 1's payoffs are listed first. For example, if Player 1 chooses to contribute and Player 2 chooses to not contribute, then their respective payoffs are 2 and 4.

19. A mixed strategy is one in which a player chooses to play pure strategies according to some preset set of probabilities. In this case, Player 1 chooses to contribute one-third of the time and not to contribute two-thirds of the time.

20. The reader should note that if Player 1 chooses any other mixed strategy, Player 2 would be better off playing a pure strategy.

21. For reasons of brevity, we will not consider mixed strategy equilibria at this point.

22. In Figure 2.4, the payoffs are listed with Player 2's first and then Player 1's.

23. In order to note the contrast between the equilibria when Player 1 goes first and when Player 2 goes first, we have chosen to represent the equilibria with Player 1's strategy first and then Player 2's strategy. This is unorthodox, but it allows us to illustrate the difference in the equilibria.

24. The first case is considered above when we introduced the concept of Bayesian Nash equilibrium.

25. See the first part of the definition of perfect Bayesian equilibrium.

26. We can, of course, eliminate any mixed strategies for Player 1 if she is a Type II player since such a player has a dominant strategy.

27. This mixed strategy was chosen because it is the one that forms part of an equilibrium in the standard game of Chicken. This is the game that is being played if Player 1 is a Type I player.

28. This mixed strategy equilibrium is calculated by setting $E_1(\text{contribute}_1) = E_1(\text{not contribute}_1)$ since this is a symmetric game.

29. Of course, we are not modelling this last situation.

30. While this may seem unreasonable now, look what happened to AMC. Then again, GM never made the Pacer.

31. The notation and characterizations benefit from those presented in Binmore (1992).

32. Since the topic of discount rates will be addressed in the following section, this formulation does not include a discount rate.

33. Of course, there are other possible equilibria. These would arise from players playing contingent strategies that results in both players playing defect in each round.

34. The entire set of strategies given different uses of prior history yields over two million uses of history to set a strategy. See Binmore (1992, pp. 349–351) for an example in a two-stage game.

35. Live for the day.

36. It is named the Folk theorem because its authorship cannot be attributed to any one individual or sets of individuals.

37. Binmore (1992), gave an eloquent mathematical and verbal treatment of the Folk theorem.

38. A helter-skelter strategy where these components are blended in a blender would also qualify. The Ordeshook definition does reign in a technical sense—any finite sequence that has these components in any order is a Nash equilibrium. We

choose to emphasize this particular order as being more understandable to us. In any helter-skelter strategy, it is hard to see how cooperation may occur except by accident. Of course, there always are those perverse organizations where beneficial actions are punished and harmful actions are rewarded. We all know of them and, by the Folk theorem, they may be a Nash equilibrium too. Except for the oddly perverse situations, our attention should be focused on more understandable and beneficial sequences.

39. Since the payoffs are symmetric, we assume the same mix of strategies across players, allowing us to calculate the mixed strategy Nash equilibrium.

40. 0.1367 can also be expressed as $\frac{4}{5} - \frac{1}{5}\sqrt{11}$.

41. See Gates and Humes (1997, pp. 103–104) for a discussion regarding very large N-player games. Here we restrict our analysis to N-player games with a sufficiently small number of players so as to preserve the strategic nature of the game. Also see von Neumann and Morgenstern (1944).

42. See Taylor and Ward (1982) or Taylor (1987) for applications to public goods in general. In our example, lobbying is a public good for the automobile producers, but it may not be a public good for the general public.

43. See Taylor (1987) for a similar analysis.

44. As noted in Chapter 2, by setting these two expectations equal to one another, we establish a point of indifference for a player. The mixed strategy then reflects this point of indifference between two choices.

45. The binomial expression allows us to take into account the potential number of subsets of a population, N, that are just big enough to make player i a critical participant. Such an expression allows us to account for the size of k with respect to N.

46. We do not assume that the sizes of N and k affect the probability of other players contributing or shirking.

47. Refer back to Chapters 1 and 3, where we examine the role of reputation in games and repeated games. Also see Selten (1978), Kreps and Wilson (1982), Milgrom and Roberts (1982), Trockel (1986), Calvert (1987), and Alt, Calvert, and Humes (1988).

48. These terms are borrowed from the popular version of the Chicken game called the Hawk and Dove game.

REFERENCES

ALT, J., CALVERT, R. L., and HUMES, B. D. (1988) "Reputation and hegemonic stability: A game theoretic analysis." *American Political Science Review* 82: 445–466.

ARROW, K. J. (1951) *Social Choice and Individual Values.* New York: Wiley.

AXELROD, R. (1980a) "Effective choice in the Prisoners' Dilemma." *Journal of Conflict Resolution* 24: 3–25.

AXELROD, R. (1980b) "More effective choice in the Prisoners' Dilemma." *Journal of Conflict Resolution* 24: 379–403.

AXELROD, R. (1981) "The emergence of cooperation among egoists." *American Political Science Review* 75: 306–318.

AXELROD, R. (1984) *The Evolution of Cooperation.* New York: Basic Books.

BINMORE, K. (1992) *Fun and Games: A Text on Game Theory.* Lexington, MA: D.C. Heath.

BRAMS, S. J. (1985) *Superpower Games: Applying Game Theory to Superpower Conflict.* New Haven, CT: Yale University Press.

BRAMS, S. J., and KILGOUR, M. D. (1988) *Theory and National Security.* New York: Basil Blackwell.

CALVERT, R. L. (1987) "Reputation and legislative leadership." *Public Choice* 55: 81–119.

COHEN, R. E. (1995) *Washington at Work.* Needham Heights, MA: Allyn & Bacon.

FEARON, J. (1994) "Signalling versus the balance of power and interests." *Journal of Conflict Resolution* 38: 236–269.

FINK, E. C., HUMES, B. D., and SCHWEBACH, V. L. (1997) "The size principle and the strategic basis of an alliance: Formalizing intuitions." *International Interactions* 22: 279–294.

FUDENBERG, D., and MASKIN, E. (1986) "The Folk theorem in repeated games with discounting or with incomplete information." *Econometrica* 54: 533–554.

GATES, S., and HILL, J. S. (1997) "Democratic accountability and governmental innovation in the use of non-profit organizations." *Policy Studies Review* 14: 000–000.

GATES, S., and HUMES, B. D. (1997) *Games, Information, and Politics: Applying Game Theoretic Models to Political Science.* Ann Arbor: University of Michigan Press.

GIBBONS, R. (1992) *Game Theory for Applied Economists.* Princeton: Princeton University Press.

HARGREAVES HEAP, S., and VAROUFAKIS, Y. (1995) *Game Theory: A Critical Introduction.* London: Routledge.

HARSANYI, J. (1967) "Games of incomplete information played by Bayesian players." *Management Science* 14: 159–182, 320–334, 486-502.

66

KREPS, D. M., and WILSON, R. (1982) "Reputation and incomplete information." *Journal of Economic Theory* 27: 253–279.

LUCE, R. D., and RAIFFA, H. (1957) *Games and Decisions: Introduction and Critical Survey*. New York: Wiley & Sons.

MAYNARD SMITH, J. (1982) *Evolution and the Theory of Games*. Cambridge: Cambridge University Press.

MAYNARD SMITH, J., and PRICE, G. R. (1973) "The logic of animal conflict." *Nature* 246(2): 15–18.

MILGROM, P., and ROBERTS, J. (1982) "Predation, reputation, and entry deterrence." *Journal of Economic Theory* 27: 280–312.

MORROW, J. (1989) "Capabilities, uncertainty, and resolve: A limited information model of crisis bargaining." *American Journal of Political Science* 33: 941–972.

MORROW, J. (1994) *Game Theory for Political Scientists*. Princeton: Princeton University Press.

MYERSON, R. (1991) *Game Theory: Analysis of Conflict*. Cambridge, MA: Harvard University Press.

NICHOLSON, M. (1989) *Formal Theories in International Relations*. New York: Cambridge University Press.

ORDESHOOK, P. C. (1986) *Game Theory and Political Theory*. Cambridge: Cambridge University Press.

ORDESHOOK, P. C. (1992) *A Political Theory Primer*. London: Routledge.

OYE, K. A. (ed.) (1986) *Cooperation Under Anarchy*. Princeton: Princeton University Press.

POWELL, R. (1987) "Crisis bargaining, escalation, and MAD." *American Political Science Review* 81: 717–735.

RASMUSEN, E. (1989) *Games and Information*. Cambridge: Basil Blackwell.

SCHELLING, T. (1966) *Arms and Influence*. Cambridge, MA: Harvard University Press.

SCHELLING, T. (1978) *Micromotives and Macrobehavior*. New York: Norton.

SCHWELLER, R. (1993) "Tripolarity and the Second World War." *International Studies Quarterly* 37: 73–107.

SELTEN, R. (1978) "The chain-store paradox." *Theory and Decision* 9: 127–159.

SNYDER, G. H. (1971) "'Prisoner's Dilemma' and 'Chicken' models in international politics." *International Studies Quarterly* 15: 66–103.

SNYDER, G. H., and DIESING, P. (1977) *Conflict Among Nations*. Princeton: Princeton University Press.

TAYLOR, M. (1976) *Anarchy and Cooperation*. London: Wiley.

TAYLOR, M. (1987) *The Possibility of Cooperation*. Cambridge: Cambridge University Press.

TAYLOR, M., and WARD, H. (1982) "Chickens, whales, and lumpy goods: Alternative models of public goods provision." *Political Studies* 30: 350–370.

TROCKEL, W. (1986) "The chain-store paradox revisited." *Theory and Decision* 21: 163–179.

VON NEUMANN, J., and MORGENSTERN, O. (1944) *Theory of Games and Economic Behavior*. Princeton: Princeton University Press.

ZAGARE, F. (1984) *Game Theory. Concepts and Applications*. Sage University Papers Series on Quantitative Applications in the Social Sciences, 07-41. Thousand Oaks, CA: Sage.

ZAGARE, F. (1985) "Towards a reconciliation of game theory and the theory of mutual deterrence." *International Studies Quarterly* 29: 155–170.

ABOUT THE AUTHORS

EVELYN C. FINK is Assistant Professor of Political Science at University of Nebraska–Lincoln. She has taught courses in game theory at Dartmouth College. Her primary research concerns the relationship between institutional change and party politics. She has published numerous articles in scholarly journals.

SCOTT GATES is Associate Professor of Political Science at Michigan State University. He has taught courses in game theory at Michigan State University and the Norwegian University of Science and Technology. His major area of research is the empirical testing of propositions derived from game-theoretic models. He has published numerous articles in scholarly journals. He is also the co-author (with John Brehm) of *Working, Shirking, and Sabotage: Bureaucratic Response to a Democratic Public* (1997) and (with Brian D. Humes) *Games, Information, and Politics: Applying Game Theoretic Models to Political Science* (1997).

BRIAN D. HUMES is Associate Professor of Political Science at University of Nebraska–Lincoln. He has taught courses in game theory at Michigan State University and the University of Nebraska–Lincoln. His primary research interest concerns the development of legislative rules. He has published numerous articles in scholarly journals. He is also a co-author (with Scott Gates) of *Games, Information, and Politics: Applying Game Theoretic Models to Political Science* (1997).

Camden College Library